SECOND THOUGHTS ON REGIONAL POLICY

Graham Hallett

First published June 1981
by Centre for Policy Studies
8 Wilfred Street, London SW1

Typeset and printed by Orchard & Ind Ltd, Northgate, Gloucester.

Contents

Preface

I have taken this opportunity to give a brief review of the present state of regional policy in the United Kingdom and, in particular, refer to the relationship between the academic study of regional economics and the development of regional policy, which have tended to drift apart in recent years. Administrators, politicians, and journalists have increasingly recognised that a change has taken place in "the regional problem" with which policy has, in one way or another, been concerned since the 1930s. The traditional view of the problem as that of a rich, over-employed South-East and a poor, under-employed, contracting "rest", no longer corresponded with the facts; this realisation has been heightened by the publicity given to the economic problems of the "inner areas" of London and Birmingham. Rather surprisingly, many regional economists have been slow to appreciate this change, so that their analyses and prescriptions have, I suggest, often become irrelevant and even misleading.

This situation is not confined to regional economics. In the neophiliac academic atmosphere of the post-war era, many new and pretentious schools of economics – neo-Keynesianism, development economics, cost-benefit analysis etc. – have enjoyed brief booms before being forced to undertake agonising reappraisals. Regional economics – in its traditional post-war form – seems due for a similar re-appraisal.

This essay is a sequel to *Regional Policy for Ever?* (Institute of Economic Affairs, 1973), and has been written at the suggestion of a distinguished Professor of Politics who found *Regional Policy for Ever?* useful for teaching purposes. Other teachers might be surprised to find that the two booklets together constituted a cost-effective intermediate text on British and European Economic Community regional policy, as well as tracts for the times.

This essay was written before the change of government, but I have added a Postscript to take account of the latest changes.

Cardiff, March 1981

Second Thoughts on Regional Policy

The Background: The Barlow Report

To read a book which begins 'The first sound in the morning was the clumping of the mill-girls' clogs down the cobbled street' and then goes on to complain about unemptied chamber pots, is to evoke a vanished world. The book is George Orwell's *The Road to Wigan Pier,* published in 1937. It was into this world that British "regional policy" was born. At that time there was an incomparably sharper regional division than today – between the "distressed areas" of South Wales, Merseyside, Tyneside, or Glasgow and the quite prosperous Midlands and Southern England. This division underlay the analysis of the *Barlow Report on the Distribution of the Industrial Population* which was published in 1940 and was based on the situation in the 1930s. Barlow argued that the problems of congested and depressed areas were two sides of the same coin, and that on economic, social and strategic grounds there should be a more balanced distribution of new industries. One of the Report's arguments – the need for a distribution of population which would be best capable of surviving aerial attack – played no role in subsequent British policy, but the Report did profoundly influence post-war policy, and established the "black and white" view of regional policy; the "black" areas being under-employed and the "white" areas being over-employed.

The idea of steering industry to the "distressed areas", was one which commanded widespread support, including my own. But there was an alternative view put, in her characteristic way, by Jane Jacobs.

> Today, only two cities in all of Britain remain economically vigorous and prosperous. One is London. The second is Birmingham. The others have stagnated one by one, much as Manchester did, like so many lights going out. British town planners, ironically, have regarded London and Birmingham as problems, because they are places in which much new work is added to old and thus cities that persist in growing.[1]

Like much of Miss Jacob's writing, that seems to me more thought-provoking than strictly true. Nevertheless, the unforeseen changes which have occurred since 1940 do suggest that planners cannot completely control the geography of employment, and that an excessively restrictive policy in the Midlands and

South-East may have damaged the seed-beds of industrial innovation. Even if Britain had the small-firm vigour which has created "Silicon Valley" in California, would it ever have obtained Industrial Development Certificates and planning permission?

Surveys of British Regional Policy
The two main books on British post-war regional policy are *Regional Policy in Britain* by Dr Gavin McCrone (1969) and *The Framework of Regional Economics in the UK* by Professor A. J. Brown (1973). Dr McCrone's book gave an excellent narrative account of the origin and progress of regional policy in all its aspects. Looking back now, when the growth rate in the Shetlands is five times the national average and many inner London boroughs have unemployment rates double the national average, one's perspective may be slightly different, but that is with the benefit of hindsight. Professor Brown's book was the outcome of a major research project undertaken by the National Institute of Economic and Social Research. It sought to give a more quantified analysis of the changes in the regional pattern, and of the role of regional policy in them, and is certainly an important source of information. By 1973, however, a few questioning voices were being raised. Was an approach which ignored the economic differences between Camberwell, Slough and Canterbury, or between Glasgow's East End, East Kilbride, and Aberdeen; which treated the "South-East Region" or "Scotland" as more or less homogenous entities, still relevant? Professor Brown concludes:

> In the last analysis, the need for regional policy is not simply a regrettable aspect of a temporary economic sickness – a view that the British have been disposed to take of their economic problems for at least fifty years. It is a normal part of the life of any economic community that likes (or even tolerates) change, but has the humanity to recognise that the economy was made for man and not man for the economy. (p.347)

This is a view which would command widespread assent (including mine) if "regional policy" were interpreted in the broad sense of, say, "spatial economic policy", thus including the effects of economic change on towns, villages or urban districts. But this is not the sense in which the term "regional policy" is normally used in British discussion – or in Professor Brown's book. "Regional policy" in the UK has been concerned with economic differences between the "Standard Regions" or areas of similar size – in particular, the difference between the North and West, and the Midlands and South-East. One can certainly agree with Professor Brown that British economic problems are not a temporary sickness. But might not "regional policy", and "the regional problem" at which it has been directed, be aspects of one particular economic sickness which was temporary in the sense that it took three decades for the symptoms to decline to a level which might reasonably be considered acceptable, given that the patient is unfortunately also suffering from several far more severe complaints? Perhaps Professor Brown's authoritative study should be regarded more as a summing-up of a past era than as a guide to future policy.

There is also a "Glasgow school" of regional economics which is "institutional" as well as "quantitative", pays due regard to international comparisons, and is concerned with urban as well as regional problems.[2] Another approach is represented by C. H. Lee's *Regional Economic Growth in the United Kingdom since the 1880s* (1971) which suggests that, although there are ebbs and flows between regions in population, employment and income, the long-run changes are much smaller than one might have imagined before studying the figures. But these studies are old-fashioned in the sense that they have a historical perspective, and are reluctant to give precise forecasts. They have received less attention than studies which, by correlating changes in investment grants with regional employment, can estimate the effects of the grants to the nearest thousand persons employed, or are able to predict that the number of registered unemployed persons in the UK in 1990 will be 4,623,000 – unless import controls are introduced.[3]

General theories

The studies which have attracted most attention are those which explain regional differences in terms of one general theory and are, therefore, able to reach striking, and often quantifiable, conclusions. Examples are Professor Gunnar Myrdal's theory of "cumulative causation", and Marxist and "Keynesian" theories of regional economics. Professor Myrdal suggests that regional differences, once established, become increasingly wide in the absence of government intervention: regions which have failed to take off are unable to do so, and emigration of the most enterprising labour continually weakens their economic potential.[4] It seems clear from any review of long-run regional change that there are indeed periods when regions, and districts, experience this type of downward spiral. It also seems clear that downward, or upward, spirals do not last forever. (If they did, "developed" countries would have larger regional differences than "less developed" countries. The reverse is the case.) In recent years the difficulty has been in distinguishing the effects of economic policy and those of market forces. But it seems clear that the shift of economic activity in the United States from New York (once "Big Apple") to the "sun belt" has not been primarily the result of government policy, and that the oil boom which has transformed much of the east coast of Scotland was unforeseen in the regional planning of the 1960s. Economic activity does not keep on piling up in one part of a country for ever. Indeed, the experience of London and Rotterdam in the 1970s suggests that, by the time that

3

governments become worried about over-concentration, decentralisation is often well under way.

Perhaps the idea of cumulative causation is more applicable to urban districts than to regions. There has certainly been a cumulative downward spiral in inner city districts such as New York, London or Liverpool. Even here, there is a need for a historical perspective: the ugly and tendentious term "gentrification" indicates that there can be counter-movements. Moreover, the implication that market forces have harmful polarising consequences, which state action corrects, hardly fits all the facts; as the British "inner area" studies bring out well, the plight of these areas, although having its origin in geographical changes, has been aggravated by official policies.[5] Thus the concept of "cumulative causation" is useful, provided it is not pushed too far. There *are* upward and downward spirals in regions and districts and, if legislators learn to understand trends better than they have in fact usually done, government policy can play a useful moderating role. But the way this concept has been put forward in the academic discussion of regional policy has probably been more misleading than helpful.

Another influential school of thought in the academic study of cities and regions has been Marxism.[6] On the Marxist interpretation, the regional (and urban) problem is caused by capitalism; peripheral regions are exploited by the interlocking state/business interests at the centre, even in the absence of explicit imperialist suppression, as in Ulster. This thesis deserves closer examination than I can give it now. I suggest below that, in Great Britain at least, there is now no clear-cut and serious "regional problem" to explain. Ulster, on the other hand, does represent a regional problem, and one with a political background, which is indeed British imperialism – of the sixteenth and seventeenth centuries.

The Quantifiers

An even more academically influential school is based on macro-economic theory or "Keynesianism" which bears only a tenuous relation to the views of Lord Keynes. This approach to regional policy has been developed in its most explicit and rigid form at the very time when, as a national policy "Keynesianism" has been in decline.[7] It is an aspect of Professor Brown's eclectic approach but is mainly associated with the "New Cambridge" economists D. Moore and J. Rhodes.[8] A recent textbook of regional economics, by two economists from Lancaster University, is more sophisticated and cautious in its correlation of time-series, but adopts basically the same approach[9] which starts from the assumption that regional differences in unemployment reflect different levels in the effective demand for labour, which can be adjusted by shifting investment from the "white" to the "black"

4

areas. At the same time, full employment in the "white" area can be maintained by the management of aggregate demand. Thus if "regional policy" creates extra jobs in the "black" region, this represents a *net increase* in jobs, not a transfer of jobs within the country[10]. (A more recent conclusion of the "New Cambridge School" is that the maintenance of full employment through demand management requires the imposition of extensive import controls).

The effect of regional policy is measured by:

(a) a correlation of changes in the level of aid and the number of plant moves the development areas;

(b) a 'shift-share' analysis of employment in development areas. National growth rates are applied to the industrial structure of development areas and if – as has recently been the case – the development areas have shown a higher growth of employment than this hypothetical level, it is assumed that the difference is the result of regional policy.

Both methods, like many macro-economic theories lacking a micro-economic basis, are open to the question: 'When A and B happen more or less simultaneously, how is one to know that B is the consequence of A, and not of C, D or E?'[11] There was certainly a large number of moves to development areas between 1945 and 1949, followed by a ten-year trough, and a recovery after 1960. Professor Brown concludes that there is a good correlation between the "strengthening" of regional policy in the 1960s and the number of moves, whether the effect is assumed to be immediate, or with a time-lag of two years. But is it realistic to assume that firms decide to move immediately increased regional aids are announced, or even after two years? The extremely limited amount of evidence available on firms' decision-making stresses the importance of pressures which build up in a plant over the years and eventually set in motion the quest for a new site.[12] Could not the "U-curve" of moves be explained in terms of two quite different "waves": the immediate post-war moves resulting from labour shortages in the South-East and Midlands, combined with more available labour and factory space in the development areas, the 1960s "wave" being the outcome of the steadily increasing pressures in inner London, etc., alongside the growing accessibility of some of the Development Areas as a result of motorway construction, the "peace" phase in Ulster before 1968, and other changes unrelated to regional policy? All one can say is that, in the absence of substantial information on industrial locational decision-making, the correlation analysis of time series is a slender basis for assessing causal relationships.

5

The same criticism can be applied to the "shift share" analysis. Professor Brown is on sound ground when he states that:

> *something* other than structure and changes in the characteristic performance of industries as such caused the four high-unemployment regions to improve their employment growth rate in relation to the rest of the country . . . (op.cit., p318)

His further conclusion that it was probably the result of changes in regional aid cries out for micro-economic verification. One study of factory closures in south-east London suggests that the closures of the 1970s may have been the delayed results of policies adopted in the 1960s – not so much regional incentives as town planning policies hostile to small businesses in London.[13] A similar emphasis on the effects of comprehensive redevelopment, congested roads, lack of skilled labour, etc., is found in both the inner area studies and a report by a director of one of the leading industrial development firms.[14] This emphasis, in studies at district level, on the influence of the local social and industrial climate, with time-lags of ten years or more, undermines the whole body of regional macro-economic analysis based on the more or less simultaneous correlation of changes in national policy and regional employment.

Moreover, the assumption – made most explicitly by Messrs. Moore and Rhodes – that full employment is being (or can be) maintained in the non-assisted areas, and that unemployment in the assisted areas can be cured simply by increasing job opportunities, is one which has been open to serious question in the 1970s. The certainty of "Keynesianism" that unemployment could be cured simply by expanding demand has – in some circles – given way to a realisation that there are many other considerations of a structural kind, such as a mismatch between the skills available and those required. The inner area studies, among others, have brought out the low level of general and vocational training, and its relation to unemployment in these districts. May not some of the (relatively low) inter-regional differences in unemployment rates have similar causes? It has been reported that some of the chemical plants on Teeside, in districts with some of the highest unemployment rates in the country, face the prospect of closure because of an acute shortage of skilled labour, arising partly from trade unions' refusal to allow the employment of re-trained persons.

If constraints operate on the supply side as well as on the demand side, the assumption (made most clearly by Messrs. Moor and Rhodes) that any increase in jobs in development areas represents a *net gain* of jobs, rather than a transfer, can be called in question. There is, on any reckoning, less than full employment in the inner areas of the large cities in the non-assisted areas. Moreover, some studies of the "shift-share" type carried out in London indicate the reverse of those carried out for the development areas: the fall in employment has been greater than might have been expected from national trends, and it has been primarily due to old firms closing down and new firms not starting up. [15](This "natural decrease" in the population of firms is confirmed by all the inner area studies, and runs counter to the Marxist explanation that large corporations have caused the problems of inner areas by moving their activities). To conclude that regional policy is the sole cause of this unexplained fall in employment would be just as questionable as the Cambridge assumption that it is the sole cause of the unexplained rise in employment in the development areas. The inner area studies indicate a variety of causes; both a decline in the inherent attractiveness of inner-city locations and policies inimical to small businesses. This situation suggests that the focus of academic investigation needs to be shifted from firms' moves and regional subsidies to the dynamics of industrial growth and decline in various types of district and under various conditions – a conclusion echoed by the work of some German business economists discussed below.

The most recent official study makes use of the 'macro-economic" approach, but clearly spells out the various assumptions that are made and the consequent limitations of the calculations.* It ends on a distinctly "revisionist" note.

> When present methodologies are used to examine the pattern of events in the regions over the past decades, we can conclude that it is highly probable that positive regional policies have had a positive effect. What we cannot draw from the methods which have been applied is any precise indication of the nature or scale of these effects. – It would seem better to approach the wider analysis of factors promoting regional development in a more piecemeal fashion. – The significance of the urban structure, the nature of the regional industrial structure, – sources of entrepreneurship and components of employment change – the role of infrastructure – could repay further investigation. (p108, III)

The Micro-economic Approach

An alternative to the "macro-economic" approach is the "micro-economic" approach of examining what actually influences firms' decisions to move, expand, or close down. It is generally taken for granted that regional subsidies play a major role in firms' decision-making, but Government statements have implied different and, even, contradictory views on the nature of such decision-making. One of the arguments for the change from tax allowances to grants in 1965 was that firms could not understand the effect of tax allowances, although they could understand a cash payment: this may well have over-estimated managerial obtuseness. [16] More recently, Labour ministers, attacking any further changes in regional aids, suggested that large firms keep an eagle eye on subsidy arrangements and fine tune their

*Measuring the effects and Costs of Regional Incentives – Judith Marquand, Government Economic Service Working Paper 32 Dept. of Industry, February, 1980.

7

investments to any changes in them; this may perhaps exaggerate the influence of subsidies as compared with other factors.

In view of the billions of pounds spent on inducing firms to move to assisted areas (and the millions spent on economic research), the amount of information available on the extent to which this money influences firms' locational decisions is astonishingly small. It is admittedly difficult to find out what really influenced a firm's decisions. Questions on the lines 'Did regional aids influence your decision on location?' are unlikely to yield reliable information. But market researchers have known for a long time that, although people often give wildly untrue answers when asked general questions, they are surprisingly truthful when asked specific questions. Thus a study of firms' locational decisions needs to be based on detailed case-studies, of which very few are available. According to Professor Brown: 'Our best evidence on the impact of government incentives on recipients comes from the '*Inquiry into Location Motives and Experience*' (p307). But this 1971 report by the then Department of Trade and Industry was confidential, and made available specially to Professor Brown, who concluded from it that financial incentives had played a major role in firms' decision-making. This may be a reasonable inference, but to have to rely on the impressions of one scholar, however eminent and fair-minded, without being able to check his data, is hardly the most scientific of procedures.

There is fragmentary evidence for a very different conclusion – that firms base their decisions on physical factors (the site, the labour supply, communications, etc.) and regard government grants as a bonus. As one small survey puts it:

> The overall scale of assistance was almost universally praised. In the words of one managing director: 'The board could hardly believe their ears'... But a number of executives qualified their enthusiasm by wondering how long the present level of assistance would last and by stating that 'one should be able to afford it all by oneself – before all the grants and loans.'[17]

Such caution was only too justified. Since 1960 there have been changes from tax allowances to grants, to tax allowances and back again: the introduction of the Regional Employment Premium and its abolition; three major and several minor changes in assisted areas (Table 1). Any calculation made by a firm in recent years of the value of regional aids in any proposed move would have been almost bound to have proved a miscalculation. The regional aids and general subsidies may have, at least, been a useful contribution to company profits during the period when these have been squeezed by historic-cost accounting combined with inflation (although they may also, by their very existence, have contributed to the unusually low profitability of British industry).[18] But the attempt to implement regional objectives through the manipulation of subsidies has, with the data available, been like trying to catch a black cat which may not be there, in the dark.

Table I

CHANGES IN TYPES OF REGIONAL AID 1960-1978

MAJOR CHANGES

	Methods				Areas
	Investment Grants	Tax Allowances	R.E.P.	Selective Aid	
1960					Development Districts
61					
62					
63					
64					
65					
66					Development Areas
67					
68					
69					
1970			Abolition announced		
71					
72					Assisted Areas (3 tiers)
73					
74					
75					
76					
77					
78					Inner areas added
79					Assisted areas reduced

The Questioners

In the 1970s a number of researchers began to question whether the "black and white" view of the British economy was still valid. In 1971, Mr Peter Randall and I decided to write a concise history and review of regional policy in Britain and the EEC, to serve the needs of students and laymen. For various reasons, the eventual outcome was a set of *Readings* by Mr Randall, Professor E. G. West of Carleton University, Ottowa, and me representing somewhat different viewpoints.[19] Mr Randall summarised the history of British regional policy and, while broadly accepting the Barlow analysis, criticised some aspects of policy, such as the concentration on the short-term alleviation of unemployment instead of support for growth points. I was far from being an opponent of regional policy: one of my first publications being a plea for assistance to Mid-Wales.[20] But when I returned to his subject it seemed to me that a sea-change had come over the British spatial economy: that most of Britain's problems had become, on the one hand, national and, on the other hand, sub-regional (e.g. inner city problems); that the need was to make the problem districts into places where people wanted to live, and satisfactory locations for industry, rather than to force industries to move there. In defence of more stable regional subsidies, I suggested that industrialists were unlikely to rely on regional aids when none had remained unaltered for more than five years and, paraphrasing Gertrude Stein's famous last words, that it was time to re-assess the nature of British regional problems.[21]

Professor West contributed a more clear-cut analysis in a scholarly essay using the "economics of politics" approach. His basic point was that there were systematic biases in political and administrative processes, which could operate so as to benefit vocal pressure groups, or administrators and politicians themselves, rather than "the public interest." This was, surely, a point worth considering – although, when Professor West went on to argue that regional policy was *solely* an empire-building exercise, he seemed to me to be going too far.

The response

This collection of essays by a Welshman of socialist and Welsh nationalist inclinations, an Anglo-Canadian ultra-liberal, and myself somewhere in between, was treated as "the IEA view,"[22] and criticised for right-wing extremism and technical incompetence by the few economists who reviewed it. A lecturer in Mathematical Economics of Birmingham University wrote:

> In considering the justification of regional policies, and particularly of IDCs that may be provided by increasing congestion of the points of the country to which labour and industry have over recent years tended to move, both Prof. West and Dr Hallett make the fundamental and elementary mistake of asserting that the rise in property rents reflect and cater for at least a major part of congestion costs. On the contrary, the rise in rents is the result of congestion costs not being implemented in any way. [23]

My specific blunder was presumably on p.11, where I gave typical rents for new offices in various cities, and suggested that the large differences in rents between Central London and elsewhere might be expected to lead to further decentralisation. Was this really an elementary mistake?

What has happened in central London since the War has *not* been a net inflow of economic activity from other parts of the country. The growth activities were in London to start with, and began to expand. After a time some of the increased office activity moved out, as a result of a combination of market and government pressures. During such an out-movement, it is quite possible for office rents to be abnormally high (in economic parlance, for the short-term equilibrium price to be above the long-term equilibrium price). But when out-migration of business reaches a certain point – and when sentiment adjusts to the new situation – the rents of previously "prime" sites can fall sharply. This has happened in the past. 'The stability of a retail business section is most endangered when rental values have reached their highest level,' as a survey of New York pointed out in 1929.[24] A remarkably similar cycle has, in fact, taken place in the 1970s: central London office rents, after a sharp rise, have fallen, both in relation to rents elsewhere and in real terms.

Table II

TYPICAL RENTS FOR NEW OFFICES
£ PER SQ.FT. PER YEAR

	1971	*1978*	*1978* *(adjusted to)* *1971 earnings*
Central London	6.0–15.0	8 – 16	2.9 – 5.8
Croydon	2.2 – 3.5	5 – 6	1.8 – 2.2
Bristol	0.8 – 1.2	1.75 – 3.2	0.6 – 1.2
Average earnings (1971 = 100)	100	275	

Source: Location of Offices Bureau

In a symposium on planning sponsored by the Social Science Research Council, the contributors on regional policy described *Regional Policy for Ever?* as 'a short, polemical, critique of regional policy,'[25] which is demonstrably incorrect. Of the five chapters, none of Mr Randall's, and only a small part of Professor West's can be described as 'polemical.' In my three chapters, the only polemical sentences refer to the Werner Plan for European monetary union, the Roskill Commission, secrecy in British government, "big name" planning consultants, and, in particular, the 1972 Industry Act, with the increase in pressure-group-subsidies to which I predicted it would give rise; they do not refer to "regional policy," in the accepted sense, at all. (Nor, at 152 pages, is the study particularly short). No reviewer considered the merits or demerits of the *Readings* for its main purpose, a student's guide to the subject, and the academic journals did not review it, so that it became a "non-publication." The treatment by journalists was varied, but one Sunday newspaper, renowned for its defence of free speech, quoted half a sentence of mine with what I considered a misleading gloss. My efforts to obtain the publication of a letter quoting the other half of the sentence, and the sentences on either side of it, proved unavailing.

These reactions are worth mentioning only because a similar treatment of currently unfashionable views was, and still is, not uncommon in British academic book reviewing, and because they typify a rather unintellectual attitude found in certain intellectual circles. Any questioning of the assumptions of currently favoured policies (at least from a non-Marxist position) has tended to be dismissed – often in such terms as "simplistic", "extremist", "polemical", "callous" or "dated" – rather than discussed. The equating of those who suggested that there was a role in economic policy for money supply guidelines with supporters of police torture has had its counterpart in the treatment of recent questioners not only of British regional policy but of more topical and important issues. The outcome has been an essentially superficial (however "sophisticated") level of debate which has contributed to the fitful, erratic and rather botched nature of British policy-making on regional subsidies, urban renewal, land policy, local government, regional devolution and other matters affecting the spatial economy.

It must be admitted that a good academic examination of problems does not solve them. It is, for example, now widely agreed that the type of comprehensive redevelopment carried out by many British cities from the 1950s to the 1970s was unsatisfactory, and that criticisms of it were for long ignored by administrators and intellectuals.[26] The USA, during the same period, had the kind of honest debate and sound academic research on urban renewal, so singularly lacking in Britain (a difference which may not be unconnected with the fact that research sponsorship in Britain is more centralised and publicly financed than in the USA). But the USA has not – in most cases – resolved the daunting problems of its central cities. What can, however, be suggested is that an open, searching and informed discussion of problems is the first step to their solution.

Changing attitudes

The last two or three years have seen signs of changing attitudes on regional policy. "Revisionist" views by geographers and others began to appear in bank reviews in 1976[27] and subsequently spread to more popular journalism, sometimes in a form which overlooked the virtues of the "development area" approach in an uncritical enthusiasm for "selective" industrial subsidies. (Indeed, attitudes on regional policy have changed so much that the ideas which were dismissed as unacceptable in 1973 may now be dismissed on the grounds that they have been commonplace among the *cognoscenti* for at least six months. But I would argue that, whatever the prevailing view, students of this, or any other, economic topic should have some knowledge of past controversies, in order to free them from the bondage of current fashion.

The most widespread academic questioning of traditional British regional policy has taken place among geographers – whose training perhaps encourages them to see fine-grained spatial changes, such as the emergence of inner city problems, which the macro-economic approach tends to overlook. A leading questioner of the "black and white" view in recent years has been Professor Michael Chisholm.[28] His argument has essentially been that what the macro-economists have seen as *regional* differences are in fact a summation of larger *sub-regional* differences. In other words, the North West region has a higher unemployment rate than the South-East simply because it has a higher proportion of districts with high unemployment. Professor Chisholm has also stressed that the decline in employment in inner cities has been largely the result of the destruction of the habitat in which small firms used to subsist, and that the policies which have produced this result need to be reviewed. This raises an important, and until recently neglected, aspect of "regional policy" – the economic differences between districts *within* regions as normally defined.

The Inner City

During the entire post-war period, while British governments were priding themselves on the humanity underlying their regional policies, they were presiding over a process of physical and social decay in older urban areas without parallel in Europe. It has, however, an instructive parallel in the USA, which until recently was ignored. Throughout the 1950s and 1960s the predominant view among British politicians, administrators and intellectuals was that any problems in the older city districts were the result of Victorian slums which were being removed by the extensive programmes of "slum clearance" being undertaken. The problems of central cities in the USA were dismissed, not without *Schadenfreude*, as typically American. Complaints that rent control was leading to massive dereliction, that "comprehensive redevelopment" was destroying neighbourhoods, that the growth of a virtual council housing monopoly was giving rise to social problems, that conditions in the schools were deteriorating, were dismissed as reactionary nonsense, unworthy of serious consideration. Virtually no large-scale independent surveys of inner areas were financed during this period. Only in the 1970s did complaints from ordinary people begin to be taken seriously. At this stage, however, a cumulative counter-movement began: journalists began to write *exposés*, academics and politicians began to take an interest, money began to become available for independent research, and some useful studies appeared. (A flood of elaborate officially-sponsored University projects are now being initiated which, in a few years time, can be expected to confirm what any intelligent newspaper reader knows already).

The most comprehensive studies available are a series on districts in Liverpool, Birmingham and London sponsored by the Department of the Environment and carried out by professional consultants. An excellent short Ministerial summary states that:

> The chief centres of this urban deprivation include the inner areas of the major conurbations. London, Glasgow, Tyne-Wear, West Yorkshire, Greater Manchester, Merseyside and West Midlands. In 1971 they contained nearly four million people, one-fourteenth of the country's population but an eighth of its unskilled workers, a fifth of its families living in some form of housing stress and a third of its new commonwealth immigrants. - - - The picture is one of exceptional concentrations of poverty and deprivation. Even so, only a minority of those living in the inner areas are below the poverty line.[29]

Although there are differences in the scale of problems in the three areas, the striking feature of these studies is the similarity of their analysis and conclusions. Not only do the reports make clear that British inner areas face serious problems, they are also unanimous in arguing that the traditional type of slum clearance has been unsatisfactory and that "regional policies," as well as local planning policies, have often had harmful results. All three reports make points which were made years ago about American "central cities," the concentration of the poor, the unskilled and immigrants; the decay of old housing; the decline of business activity; the suffering caused by "the municipal bulldozer" combined with neglect in other fields; the failure of the schools.

In all three areas, the problems pinpointed as the most important are the poor quality of housing and the environment, and low incomes. In Liverpool, 'the most striking impression is physical decay'; one-tenth of the total area has been cleared, with the idea of building schools, open spaces or highways which have not been built, and are unlikely to be built for years. In Small Heath:

> It is the obsolescence and deterioration of the housing stock – even more than employment conditions – that have led to a 'downward' spiral. Housing conditions, rather than jobs, have determined where people live. Poor occupants of the houses have found their maintenance too costly, and the relatively better off have been able to take the option of moving out altogether. The less skilled labour force has found it more difficult to take advantage of such employment opportunities as do exist; in turn, the absence of skilled labour has made the area less attractive to employers.

The decline in employment in the three areas was in all cases initiated by structural changes which could hardly have been prevented, but has subsequently been accelerated both by the deterioration in the local environment and by mis-directed planning policies. In none of the areas was the decline caused by firms moving out, but by existing firms dying and new employment not being created. In Liverpool, the initial downturn was caused by the decline of the port and the elimination of central warehousing.

Merseyside has been a "development area" since the War, and 100,000 new manufacturing jobs have been created, but these have all been located on the edge of the conurbation. Central area employment has declined faster than population, and the rate of unemployment is several times the national average. In Small Heath, factories have become outmoded, and have closed down in disproportionate numbers. The creation of new employment in Birmingham and London has been hampered by regional policy. In Lambeth, the unemployment problem is partly the result of the run-down in local manufacturing, but also of a mis-match of job opportunities and skills. There has been a national shift from less skilled to more skilled jobs, especially in Central London, which is virtually part of the Lambeth labour market. But the Lambeth labour force is largely unskilled, and with few opportunities to acquire skills.

The three reports are agreed that the policy pursued in these areas since the 1930s – bulldozing whole streets and putting up council housing – has been unsatisfactory. The Liverpool study speaks of the 'brutal uprooting of communities' which has accelerated the exodus of skilled people. The council estates are 'poorly maintained and heavily vandalised.' It groups together council estates and rooming houses as having the worst social and environmental conditions, but also points out that the area contains considerable diversity; there are still stable working class neighbourhoods and multi-racial communities with a potential for recovery. The Small Heath study speaks of the 'avoidable misery' caused by council redevelopment; the imbalance of Birmingham's housing expenditure between new construction (which 1975/6 still took the lion's share) and the improvement of older property; and the failure of the current system of housing subsidies to help those most in need. In Lambeth, one of the main social problems is 'the

Table III

THE LABOUR FORCE IN THE INNER AREAS OF MAJOR
CONURBATIONS, 1971

Area	% of Labour Force Unskilled or Semi-Skilled
Inner Birmingham	38
Inner Manchester	35
Inner Glasgow	34
Inner Liverpool	39
National Figure	23

Source: Census of Population 1971.

Table IV

CAUSES OF INDUSTRIAL CLOSURES IN LONDON, 1966-74

Cause	% of London's job loss
Firm cutting down	23
Firm closing	50
Firm moving to assisted areas	9
Firm moving to new towns	7
Firm moving to a new location in South East	11

Source: A. Lapping, London's burning, London's burning: a survey' *The Economist* 1.Jan. 1977 p.17.

constant shifting of families, exacerbated by council redevelopment schemes and the decline in privately-rented housing.' The Lambeth report is clear that 'There is no justification for further large-scale redevelopment in Inner London. The housing gain this sought to achieve has proved illusory; such gain is better sought further out.' At the same time, it warns that not all housing is worth retaining, and that some new construction will be needed; the precise mix can be determined only on a "house-to-house" basis.

Finally, all three studies express an underlying disquiet with the organisation and attitudes of local government. The city authorities have intervened too much with "bulldozer" policies (which are largely paid for by the national government) but have otherwise devoted relatively few resources to these areas, and have neglected their employment problems. The Liverpool and Small Heath reports suggest that the city government has been remote, and insensitive to local needs. The Small Heath report comments on 'a widespread lack of confidence in the area and in its government', but is reluctant to advocate a major reorganisation of local government 'so soon after the recent upheaval with its attendant increases in costs and bureaucracy'.

Just as there is a striking similarity in the diagnosis of the three reports, so there is *mutatis mutandis* a striking similarity in their proposals. All believe that improvements are possible and that, as the Small Heath report puts it, 'What is essential is that action to set revitalisation under way is taken now while retrieval is still possible'. But all the reports accept that policy must accept the economic forces which have led to a decline in inner city population and employment, and should concentrate on encouraging adjustments to a new equilibrium.

All three reports outline similar policies for (a) economic development, (b) the alleviation of poverty, (c) education and training, (d) the reform of housing policy, and (e) the decentralisation of administration. In most cases, the policies that require change are national rather than local. All the reports advocate measures to attract or retain viable employment, especially in small firms, which fit better into the close grained texture of old districts. The reports for Birmingham and London advocate the abolition of Industrial Development Certificates and Office Development Permits. All three reports advocate a rethinking of planning policies which, in the pursuit of an excessive segregation of housing and workplaces, have contributed to the flight of industry. They also advocate a policy of making land available for new industrial premises, or rehabilitating old premises.

All three reports express a dissatisfaction with the performance of the existing welfare state and attach high priority to alleviating poverty by direct cash transfers. The third element in the suggested programme is training and education to reduce the mismatch between job opportunities and available skills. The Lambeth report advocates more emphasis in schools on 'basic academic skills and vocational preparation' and points out that opportunities for school-leavers to undertake vocational training are very limited compared with those in other European countries.[30]

The fourth element concerns housing policy. All three suggest that the administration of council housing is unsatisfactory, being too remote and bureaucratic. In the same vein, the Lambeth report stresses that if, as is likely under existing policies, private tenancy is largely eliminated, it should be replaced by "social ownership" based on a variety of non-profit enterprises (which have lower costs than councils'), and that the level of "fair rents", which now bears no relation to costs, should be raised by means of an explicit formula giving a fair rate of return on capital, which would then be indexed for inflation. Besides assisting housing associations, this would enable some resident landlords to remain. The reports all favour small-scale improvements rather than massive schemes. The Lambeth report points out that the social and environmental dangers of having large impersonal areas of space which have been one of the hallmarks of public housing projects: it advocates the concept of "defensible space": 'Every space should look as though it belonged to someone', or be supervised. Finally, the reports suggest that the regeneration of the inner areas requires a more decentralised system of public administration, in which local people do not feel, as they do now, that their views are ignored, and that City Hall wishes to forget about them.

A minor but possibly further contributory factor – not mentioned in the inner area studies – concerns local government finance. The current system – based largely on grants from the central government – has probably aggravated rather than alleviated the problems of inner city areas. The grants are calculated according to an extremely complicated and obscure formula which is supposed to reflect both a local authority's "needs" and its "resources" (in terms of rateable value). The handful of independent specialists who have mastered the intricacies of the system are unanimous in their view that it has not fulfilled its stated objectives very well. The "needs" element tends to be calculated on a *per capita* basis, using past expenditure patterns: thus the inner areas, which have been losing economically active people, tend to suffer. The " resources" element is based on rateable value which – partly because of the obsolete and hence artificial letting value by which rates are calculated – no longer reflects the level of local income. As a result, inner areas have to charge higher rates (per economically active person) for services which are often poorer. A more rational and clear-cut system of local government finance would – from the point of view of 'the public good' – be preferable to "partnership" arrangements and special payments from the central government. Why have less satisfactory policies in fact been adopted? The American "public choice" school explains this type of phenomenon in terms of the costs and benefits to politicians, under the prevailing political constitution. Politicians are not concerned solely with "the public good", but also with their own survival and advancement (which they may come to equate with the public good).[31]

A general reform of local government finance would bring little direct political benefit to a government: "generous" grants to specific authorities do (or are

Table V

RATES PER ECONOMICALLY ACTIVE PERSON
IN LONDON, 1973-74

	Rates per economically active person £
Selected Inner London Boroughs	
Islington	183
Lambeth	131
Southwark	152
Tower Hamlets	199
Selected Outer London Boroughs	
Bromley	115
Harrow	118
Redbridge	118
Richmond	121

Source: N. Falks and H. Martinos, *Inner City*, Fabian Research Paper 320, Fabian Society, 1975.

thought to); hence the adoption of policies which leave much to be desired. This is not a counsel of despair. It does, however, imply that it is as misguided to trust in the benevolence of democratic governments as, in the seventeenth century, it was to trust in the benevolence of princes.

Is capitalism to blame?

The conclusion of the inner area studies is, in effect, that the decline of these areas does not have a single cause, but several mutually interacting causes, originating in unavoidable economic changes but aggravated by misguided government policies. This analysis is rejected by many leading academics. The academic study of housing policy in Britain has been dominated in recent years by the "social administration" school founded by the late Professor Titmuss. This school – which it seems fair to say – regards council housing, rent control and "slum clearance" as "good things", shades over into various types of academic Marxism which have attracted a considerable following in urban sociology and urban geography, as well as a more populist type of Marxist analysis which underlies many "community" movements.[32]

An example of an intellectually sophisticated Marxist analysis of urban problems is provided by Professor David Harvey's *Social Justice and the City* (Edward Arnold 1973), which received almost unprecedented acclaim from the academic journals.

> A penetrating analysis of contemporary urbanism which may indeed be the signal change of direction in geographic thought... ...without doubt one of the most significant contributions to geographical thought to emerge in the last two decades, ...a refreshingly new analysis. ...one of the most fertile and fruitful scholars working in the field of urban studies.

Professor Harvey's analysis relies on the concept of "use value", which Marx took over from an aside by Adam Smith, and on Marx's concept of "absolute rent". It is not, I hope, a misinterpretation of an elaborate argument to say that he interprets the ghetto as a consequence of exploitation by the small capital-owning class, of which the building societies, etc., are the instruments. He considers the state of "central cities" throughout the USA to be confirmed of this thesis 'under the capitalist mode of production.' This type of capitalist exploitation is eliminated under a communist system, where the allocation of housing takes place through an administrative instead of a market system, and "absolute rent" is eliminated.

I cannot do more in this essay than comment briefly on whether urban decay always, and only, accompanies "capitalism". In any comparison of cities in "developed" countries – in particular, those of Western Europe, Canada and the USA – the differences are as striking as the similarities. Incipient decay is universal: there are clearly general tendencies at work. On the other hand, the extent varies enormously, from a slight shabbiness (which may be no bad thing, as it can accompany cheap housing) to the serious physical and social decay of New York or Liverpool. The most serious decay is present in the USA – especially the East Coast cities – and the UK. Nothing on a comparable scale is found in Canada or European countries such as West Germany, the Netherlands or Scandinavia; the problems are somewhat more serious in some French and Italian cities. It seems difficult to explain this variation in terms of the Marxist analysis. Canada is institutionally similar to the USA. It does have stricter town planning controls, but these are accompanied by higher land and property prices, i.e. "absolute rent", the symptom, in the Marxist view, of capitalist exploitation.

The most striking case, however, is the UK, which has problems virtually as serious as the USA and an incomparably more serious problem than West Germany, Benelux or Scandinavia. But the UK, in the field of housing and urban landownership, is not more "capitalist" than other countries: on the contrary, the severity of rent control, the contraction of private rented housing, and the extent of municipal ownership of land and housing in inner areas, is greater than in other European countries. The Marxist explanation does not, therefore, seem to explain international differences very well. On the other hand, the American experience goes against those who would lay the blame for the British situation *solely* at the door of rent control and "the municipal bulldozer". International comparisons would seem to reinforce the view in the "inner area" studies that several influences are involved, and that no single explanation is adequate. Urban and regional economists would do well to heed a plea made by an engineer some years ago for 'no more general theories'.[34]

All countries have experienced a movement of industry out of inner areas, and the problems of ageing housing. In addition there are many other, sometimes self-inflicted, problems which vary in intensity from country to country and city to city.

> ...next to bombing, rent control seems in many cases to be the most efficient technique so far known for destroying cities, as the housing situation in New York City demonstrates.[35]

Other factors include policies on immigration, urban renewal, transport, education, non-profit participation in housing and local government. Some policies encourage decay, others retard it, and encourage regeneration; the mix of policies varies from country to country. The relative severity of urban decay in the UK can perhaps be explained by the hypothesis that, whereas some other countries have adopted policies conducive to urban decay in one or two fields, the UK has adopted them in nearly all.

Policy for the Inner Cities

The Labour Government's response to the changed attitudes towards inner cities was given in the White Paper *Policy for the Inner Cities* (Cmnd. 6845) published in June 1977. Its acceptance of the serious condition of these areas, and the need to arrest their decline represented an important change. On the other hand, the analysis of the areas' problems was cursory, and the detailed policy recommendations bitty and obscure, revealing, to those experienced in textual exegesis, differing attitudes within the Government and civil service.

The "nature of the problem" was analysed – reasonably enough – as a loss of jobs in traditional industries, physical decay and a concentration of poor and socially handicapped people. The discussion of the causes of decay, however, was far from searching.

> The bulldozers have done their work, but the rebuilding has lagged behind. Sometimes this has been caused by changes of plan as more people left the cities than expected. In other instances, it has resulted from reductions in the allocation of resources, central and local. Whatever the explanation, there is a wide extent of vacant land in some inner areas, mainly in public ownership: and there is much under-used land and property, with shops boarded up and sites and buildings neglected.

The possibility that comprehensive re-development schemes, planning powers exercised by councils hostile to private ownership of housing or business, and rent control, may have contributed to the problems was not explicitly conceded, although it seems implicit in some statements. Public investment 'must be on a more human scale, with less disruption of community ties'. 'The resources of small and medium size firms are essential if real progress is to be made and the diversity and vitality, for so long characteristic of inner cities, is to be restored'. 'Controls over the expansion of light industry in residential areas can be relaxed where this can be done without serious objection on noise or nuisance grounds.' 'The state of the private rented sector is especially significant in some inner areas. The current review of the Rent Acts will be particularly relevant to the needs of these parts of cities' (a hope which anyone who has studied the history of British rent legislation must view with some scepticism).

On the other hand, the "Conclusions" echoed the historically questionable view that post-war policies have helped to clear up the mess left by the Victorians. 'The current state of the inner area has its roots in social and economic events reaching to the last century and beyond. Much has been done to ease their problems since the Second World War...'.

The preliminary discussion reached the very reasonable conclusion that, although 'some of the changes which have taken place are due to social and economic forces which could be reversed only with great difficulty or at unacceptable cost,' nevertheless, 'the inner parts of our cities ought not to be left to decay'. Vacant or under-utilised land in these areas should not be abandoned, and it should be possible to 'achieve a more balanced structure of jobs and population within our cities'. The specification proposals were that more money should be channelled to the inner areas, at the expense of New Towns, and that small-scale industrial development should be encouraged rather than discouraged. 'Partnership arrangements' were to be entered into by the central government with a number of local authorities (Birmingham, Liverpool, Manchester, Glasgow and Lambeth and the docklands areas in London) under which money be provided and a 'unified approach' to inner areas adopted. Local authorities would be given money and powers to build advance factories and provide initial 'rent holidays' for incoming firms. They were to be encouraged to improve employment prospects by allocating more land to industrial and commercial activities. At the same time, regional policy would be given an "intra-regional emphasis". Inner London and Inner Birmingham, instead of being "white", non-assisted areas, less favoured than the "black" or "grey" Assisted Areas, would in future be black islands in a white sea.

Enough has been said to suggest that, although official policy (in 1978) had changed, the attitudes which for a generation underlay policies now widely regarded as mistaken had not changed overnight. (It would be surprising if they had). The official view that 'slum clearance' was removing the problems of the inner city was the counterpart to the "black and white" view of the regional economy. Although official views on both issues are now changing, the White Paper gave little ground for believing that a coherent and realistic view of urban and regional problems had yet emerged. The only specific policies to be proposed were to spend more public money and relax planning restrictions on industrial development. But for new employment to emerge in the inner city there were will probably have to be radical changes in both local planning attitudes and in national policy towards small firms and the development process. Similarly, there are many aspects of current social, housing and educational policy which are particularly harmful in inner city districts where people have less opportunity to either go outside the state system or influence it. More money for the inner cities is necessary; whether by itself it will be enough seems doubtful.

The proposals in the White Paper were promptly translated into the Inner Urban Areas Act, under which "partnership" schemes with various local authorities have been established. What little information is available so far confirms the doubts prompted by the White Paper. Public expenditure in the inner cities needs to be based on a carefully considered medium-term programme (of, say, five years). But the money has, up till now, been made available on a year-to-year basis; if an authority did not spend the current year's money, it lost it. The inevitable result in some authorities has been that money has been spent on hastily conceived schemes, some of which – such as temporary school buildings – will result in increased expenditure in a few years, when fashions may have changed and less money be available. It is ironic that governments which believe in "planning" often neglect it in those aspects of public expenditure where it is most needed.[36]

So much for the inner city problems. But there are other sub-regional problems which have tended to be overlooked in the belated publicity recently given to inner cities. The closure of a large plant, for example, can have severe effects on a local community. This can happen in non-assisted as well as assisted areas, and traditional regional policy (in its restrictive aspects) can sometimes have results contrary to those intended. For example, several firms wished to set up in Corby in the 1960s but were refused IDC's, on the grounds that the local labour force was fully employed by existing enterprises, especially the large steelworks, the future of which was apparently never called in question. Now the British Steel Corporation wishes to close the works, and the town faces the prospect of becoming a new Jarrow.

Whether this closure, and that of other steelworks, is economically justified (or, more academically, whether the "concentration" strategy adopted by the British Steel Corporation in the 1960s was justified) is hard to say, given the lack of published information on costs and profits. It may well be that it is, and was. There is, however, a section of informed opinion which holds that the existing performances of the smaller works, after having been starved of capital for years, is being incorrectly compared with the marginal costs of the favoured large works, since these marginal costs are based on performance standards which the large works have rarely achieved, and are unlikely to achieve in the future. What is hardly in dispute is that the attempt in the early 1970s to institute a completely centralised management structure (with the specific aim of breaking down local loyalties) was accompanied by production difficulties which led to the British steel industry, for the first time in its history, losing a third of the home market to imports. The BSC has now reverted to a more "regional" style of management; a further step in this direction would be regional "profit centres". The case for "devolution" is not confined to politics.

Is there still a regional problem in Britain?

It seems clear that there are serious intra-regional, or sub-regional, problems in the British inner cities, as well as in towns like Corby and some other cases (some islands and some remote rural areas). But is there a *regional* problem? Regional economists usually measure regional differences in terms of unemployment rates, average incomes, migration and similar economic variables. Other indicators include the ownership of cars, central heating, washing machines, etc., the proportion of houses without the "standard amenities", the proportion of people on supplementary benefit, etc. The differences between British Standard Regions with regard to unemployment rates, average incomes per head, net migration and (as an example of various physical indicators) car ownership are shown below.

It is clear from the tables that Northern Ireland is in a class by itself, being well outside the range of the other regions in terms of income and unemployment. Northern Ireland is the British regional problem today, just as Ireland was in the nineteenth century. And, as then, the regional problem raises social, political and ideological as well as economic, issues.[37]

Table VI

UNEMPLOYMENT RATES
DECEMBER 1978

	%
Northern Ireland	11.2
British Development Areas	8.7
British Intermediate Areas	5.5
Great Britain	5.6
*Non-assisted areas: high unemployment**	
Corby	6.9
Ramsgate	7.9
Great Yarmouth	8.4
*London local authorities give estimates of over 10% for several inner London boroughs but the DOE gives no breakdown of the London total.	
Assisted areas: low unemployment	
Aberdeen	3.7
West Yorkshire Metropolitan	5.1
Powys	5.2
Greater Manchester Metropolitan	5.4
Assisted area: high unemployment	
Tyne & Wear Metropolitan	9.5
Western Isles	14.1

Source: Department of Employment Gazette, January 1979. p.51.

Table VII

REGIONAL DIFFERENCES IN THE UK

	Unemploy-ment June 1978 %	Disposable Income per head 1976 UK = 100	Internal Migration 1975-6 000s	Households owning a car %
South-East	4.0	109.7	−32	60.2
East Anglia	4.8	92.0	+18	70.5
East Midlands	4.8	97.7	+ 4	57.1
West Midlands	5.2	97.4	−19	57.5
Yorks. & Humberside	5.5	96.1	− 6	51.0
South West	6.2	96.2	+31	66.6
North West	6.9	97.4	−17	48.3
Scotland	7.6	97.5	− 5	45.1
Wales	7.9	91.4	+ 5	58.3
North	8.0	95.1	− 1	51.1
N. Ireland	11.0	84.4	n.a.	46.9

Source: Regional Economic Statistics.

Table VIII

RELATIVE UNEMPLOYMENT RATES (UK =100)

	1957	1965	1970	1972	1974	1976	1977	1978	1979
Scotland	162	200	162	168	154	121	134	134	140
North	106	187	177	166	177	129	135	145	149
Wales	162	193	150	126	142	128	131	140	140
North West	100	107	104	126	135	121	121	122	124
Yorks & Humberside	—	73	108	111	100	97	94	98	100
South West	113	107	108	89	100	110	113	108	98
East Midlands	—	60	85	79	85	83	82	82	82
East Anglia	81	87	81	76	73	84	87	82	72
West Midlands	—	60	73	95	n.a.	102	94	91	98
South East	63	60	62	58	58	72	73	68	65
UK percentage	1.6	1.5	2.6	3.8	2.6	5.8	6.2	6.2	5.7
Standard Deviation*		54.9	37.4	35.4	37.8	19.3	22.0	25.6	25.9

Source: Regional Economic Statistics.

* The standard deviation is a statistical measure of dispersion; the smaller the figure the less the "spread" of regional unemployment rates.

Table IX

AVERAGE ANNUAL NET INTERNAL MIGRATION

	1951-61	1961-71	1971-73	1973-74	1974-75	1975-76
South East	+43.8	− 3.7	−38.4	−84.9	−47.3	−31.9
(Greater London)	(−61.0)	(−98.2)	(−106.8)	(−118.2)	(−68.4)	(−71.4)
West Midland	+ 4.7	− 1.3	− 4.1	− 0.2	−13.7	−18.7
North West	−12.4	−11.4	−16.3	−22.3	−17.1	−16.7
Yorks & Humberside	− 9.6	− 7.0	− 4.0	− 0.5	− 3.4	− 5.9
Scotland	−28.2	−32.5	−19.2	+ 7.8	−19.0	− 4.8
North	− 8.0	−10.8	− 9.0	− 7.8	− 4.1	− 0.5
East Midlands	+ 3.9	+ 7.1	+16.9	+12.6	+ 6.1	+ 3.6
Wales	− 4.9	− 0.4	+ 8.4	+ 8.8	+ 6.3	+ 5.5
East Anglia	+ 2.7	+21.1	+12.6	+15.6	+19.0	+18.1
South West	+ 9.9	+22.4	+41.4	+28.5	+28.0	+30.9

Source: Regional Economics Statistics.

The Irish problems are not generally understood in other European countries, and it can hardly be claimed that British media coverage over the past ten years has always helped to illuminate it. There has been a (very unhistorical) tendency to assume that people could not hate and kill each other just because they belonged to different sects of the same religion, and that the problem must be one of a repressed minority, which could be cured by "civil rights". Only recently has it begun to be realised in the media that there is a "dual minority" problem. The Protestants are unwilling to be a minority in a united Ireland, because of a fear (however unjustified under present conditions) of Catholic oppression. The Catholics are unwilling to be a minority in Northern Ireland. Each side hates and fears the other. The partition of Ireland in 1922 left several Catholic "pockets" in the North and, although some could – and probably should – be removed by ceding territory to the Republic, others could not. In these circumstances, economic (or military) policy can have only a limited effect. The province is being massively, and probably justifiably, supported by the British Exchequer, and there is little scope for increasing the present level of support. Indeed, some of the selective aid designed to bring employment to the Catholic districts of Belfast – such as the £50m aid to DeLorean Motors – has an air of desperation about it. Without some kind of solution to the present sectarian differences in Northern Ireland, no purely economic policy is likely to solve the problem – a neither original nor optimistic conclusion. I shall therefore confine my discussion of regional differences to Great Britain in the narrow sense.

The main impression of the quoted regional differences in Great Britain is that they are small and by no means consistent. Disposable income lies in the range of 10 per cent on either side of the average. By international standards, this is very small; indeed, bearing in mind the differences in housing and transport costs (which are on average, higher in the South East than in other regions) the differences might be considered insignificant. It is noteworthy that the South-East is losing population to regions with lower average money incomes.

The average unemployment rates cover the range from 4 to 8 per cent, and the dispersion (in terms of ratios) is lower than in the 1960s or 1950s. (There has been a slight reversal since 1977 of the previous downward trend). However, these statistical unemployment rates need to be treated with considerable caution. It would, of course, be desirable to reduce unemployment rates everywhere to some "full employment" level but, just as the national unemployment problem may require some re-thinking, so may its geographical distribution. The case of the BL car factory at Speke, near Liverpool, illustrates both that investment undertaken at Government request may not by itself, create permanent employment, and that employment on the outskirts of cities may not directly affect the districts of really high unemployment in "inner areas". Another defect of concentrating on regional unemployment rates is that it distracts attention from absolute numbers: there are more unemployed in London than in Wales.

The official figures on inter-regional migration are very damaging to the "black and white" view of the British economy. They indicate that the South-East and West Midlands have been losing population in the 1970s, while the East Midlands, Wales, East Anglia and the South West have been gaining it. The traditional Scottish emigration has fallen to a low level. The only "black" area which has had steady and high emigration has been the North-West. But the inter-regional migration figures are dwarfed by the enormous and steady fall in the population of London.

It could be argued that these changes can be credited to regional policy. It may have played a role, but the regions gaining population are not generally development areas. It looks as though the migration changes are the result of substantial numbers of households and firms deciding that the disadvantages of London outweighed its advantages and moving, but generally over distances of less than a hundred miles.

Is there still a regional problem? There are certainly serious problems in older cities; some of these are in assisted areas, but Birmingham, London and some other cities are not. Britain also faces serious problems in the fields of industrial relations, vocational skills and the urban environment; these problems are similarly national, although they may be slightly more severe in some regions than in others. This complex of problems is very different from "the regional problem" which, implicitly or explicitly, has underlain policy for the past forty-five years.

The methodology of regional economics

The trouble with much recent regional economics is that it has elevated one consideration among many into an exclusive (and historically rather blinkered) dogma. Listening to a recent educational radio discussion on industrial policy, I was struck by a dialogue which went something like this:

> A. 'As this is a field in which new ideas have challenged traditional theory, I am going to ask the youngest member of our team to explain the new thinking. Will you do that, Bob?
>
> B. Yes, Bill. You see, the old economics assumed that if, for example, a factory was making a loss it should be closed down. But we know that it should be kept going because it is part of the infra-structure of the region'.

Similar arguments have often been put forward for "regional policy" although "infrastructure" is usually used with reference to roads, sewers, schools, etc. Businessmen, it is argued, by considering merely their direct costs and receipts when deciding on the location of investment, can produce a wasteful under-utilisation of resources. There is something in this argument, although it can be overdone, because the "social capital" of old industrial areas is often worn-out or obsolete, and needs replacement. A more extended version of the argument embraces industrial capital, and links up with the "job preservation" argument that it is better to keep unprofitable enterprises going than to pay unemployment benefit. But should every factory be kept in operation regardless of profitability? Profitability is not a perfect guide to resource allocation, but in industry it is not a bad one. Should the Lancashire cotton mills, or the G.E.C. Woolwich factory, or the BL No. 2 car factory at Speke, have been kept going? The preferable alternative is to produce new or improved products. In so far as the UK has been less successful than other countries in this respect, its unique system of labour practices must surely bear some responsibility, together with managerial failings. And the social consequences of any closure should of course be considered and alleviated. But if all attempts to cut costs or switch to more profitable products fail, closure can have the economic virtue of freeing at least part of the labour and capital for uses which are more profitable in both a private and a social sense. It does not follow that the factory will remain unused, although this depends on the type of building. Some multi-storey nineteenth century factories are unsuited for modern manufacturing, and it would make little sense to retain them in this use. (However, it is surprising to what an extent they have found new uses, which is pleasing anyone who admires these often fine buildings).

28

The doctrine that, in order to prevent a waste of resources, every factory, or any other fixed investment, should be kept in its existing use, or any kind of use, is based on a very static analysis. There have always been what Joseph Schumpeter called 'waves of creative destruction', and they are unlikely to have stopped now.[38] Most of the Lancashire cotton mills, or the coal-exporting docks of South Wales had, by the 1950s, ceased to be part of the region's infrastructure; they had been rendered valueless by economic change. The "infrastructure" argument (in its dogmatic form) also substitutes categorical imperatives for 'the nicely calculated lore of less or more'. In some cases, it is not so much a question of keeping or scrapping "infrastructure" but of weighing up how much can be modernised and how much has to be replaced, on the existing site or another. Thus it is often difficult to make a convincing case for regional policy solely on the basis of 'hard-nosed' economic calculations. Equally important in the thinking of the originators of British post-war regional policy were 'soft-nosed' politico-social considerations. On purely financial grounds, it might have been better to let some districts rot; this was regarded as socially and environmentally unacceptable, although it was generally accepted that *some* change was inevitable. The "infrastructure" argument (in its dogmatic form), like the "macro-economic" approach, seeks to provide a "hard-nosed", purely economic, justification for regional policy – although one which is open to question even on its own terms. By adopting this approach, British regional economists have ignored the "soft-nosed" considerations which provided the impetus for post-war policy, and which, in a different context, are likely to continue to be important.

There is thus no objective way of assessing the optimal scale of regional, or local, assistance. All one can say in general terms is that it would be absurd to try to freeze for all time the existing distribution of industry and population, but that there can be heavy costs involved in going to the other extreme and taking no account of the effect of industrial change on urban and regional development. What policies should be adopted between these two extremes is a matter for informed debate.

The 1972 'U-turn'

Although it is difficult to assess the optimal level, or geographical distribution, of regional aid, the issues are more clear-cut on the *methods* of such aid. The 1972 Industry Act represented a fundamental change not merely in economic but in constitutional policy, which was inadequately appreciated or debated during its passage. Up to 1972 (with one slight qualification) the principle had been maintained of equal treatment under the law. Whatever the arrangements for taxes or subsidies, they applied to every individual or company without discrimination. The qualification was that certain regions were treated more favourably than others. Delimiting these regions

Table X

UNOFFICIAL ESTIMATES OF THE EXCHEQUER COST OF REGIONAL POLICY (EXCLUDING TAX ALLOWANCES WHEN PAYABLE)
£m

	Mainly recoverable items	*Non-recoverable items*					
		Local Employment Acts	*Investment Grants*	*Free Depreciation*	*REP*	*SET premium*	*TOTAL*
1950-1959 Average	5.9	—	—	—	—	—	—
1960-61	44.5	6.0					6.0
1961-62	21.9	2.3					2.3
1962-63	10.0	6.2					6.2
1963-64	24.6	5.7					5.7
1964-65	23.1	17.4	—	3.0			20.4
1965-66	22.0	20.4	—	45.0			65.4
1966-67	27.6	27.8	—	25.0			52.8
1967-68	25.2	21.1	72.0	4.0	34.1		131.2
1968-69	31.6	23.4	85.0	—	101.0	25.0	234.4
1969-70	46.1	34.7	90.0	—	105.0	25.0	257.9
1970-71	35.9	31.5	90.0	—	110.0	—	234.3

Source: Memorandum by Messrs. Moore and Rhodes to the House of Commons Expenditure Committee (Trade and Industry Sub-Committee) 1973.

periodically involved discretionary decisions by the government, but of a limited kind. This remained true of the Regional Employment Premium. The abolition of the REP and the subsequent introduction of selective subsidy represented a radically different method of regional aid, the approach of the 1964 Labour Government being in this respect liberal and the approach of the 1970 Conservative Government collectivist. As Mr. Samuel Brittan puts it in a prescient essay, published before the "U-turn":

> . . . nothing better illustrates the underlying detestation of many of the 1970 breed of Conservatives of policies working through the price mechanism and impersonal market forces than their attitudes to the regions.[39]

The REP has the constitutional virtue, to an economic liberal, of being an impersonal general regulation which allowed decentralised decision-making and did not require the Government decisions in individual cases. It also had the economic virtue of providing a subsidy for labour, to offset the capital-intensive bias of investment grants. The "selective" aid introduced by the 1972 Industrial Act was, to an economic liberal, objectionable, in that it was insufficiently based on objective general principles, and thus opened the door to unlimited subsidies to any firm or industry in difficulties.

Under Section 7 of the Act, selective assistance can be given in the assisted areas, but under Section 8 it can be given in any area, and a substantial proportion has gone to non-assisted areas. Although the amount of assistance was at first small, it subsequently increased rapidly, and assistance has been given to many industries, including wool textiles, foundries, machine tools, paper and board, electronics and textile machinery, as well as individual companies ranging from British Leyland and Rolls Royce to Delorean Motors

Table XI

GOVERNMENT PREFERENTIAL ASSISTANCE TO INDUSTRY
IN THE BRITISH ASSISTED AREAS
£m

	Regional Development	Local Employment Acts	Investment Grants Differential	REP	SET Premium	Total
1968-69		50.7	89.0	103.0	25.6	273.3
1969-70		58.5	100.0	109.1	27.1	303.1
1970-71		60.8	123.5	109.1	7.4	310.4
1971-72		64.7	90.4	109.6	0.2	274.8
1972-73	8	68.6	66.9	100.6	0.2	255.3
1973-74	107	57	29	106	—	339.7
1974-75	213	40	15	154	—	473.4
1975-76	325	39	5	213	—	669.4
1976-77	408	22	2	216	—	719.9
1977-78	393	21	1	3	—	507.5

Note: 1973-74 to 1977-78. 'All figures are gross and include payments to nationalised industries. The major items of expenditure included are regional development grants, selective financial assistance under Section 7 of the Industry Act, 1972, Local Employment Act assistance, regional employment premium (which was discontinued in January, 1977) and investment grant differential (estimated).

Source: 1968-69 to 1972-73.
Memorandum submitted by the Department of Trade and Industry to the House of Commons Expenditure Committee (Trade and Industry Sub-Committee) 1973-74 to 1977-78. House of Commons Written Answer 14 March 1979, and other sources.

and Hoffman la Roche. The extent of selective assistance practised since 1974 has gone far beyond anything envisaged by the Conservative Government in 1972, but the consequences of the 1972 Industry Act could have been foreseen, and were foreseen. In hardly any other Western country could an Act embodying a change of such constitutional significance have been framed and passed in a year. It is by no means obvious that this unparalleled speed of the British legislative process (utilised even more strikingly by the succeeding Government), is a cause for congratulation.

Table XII

EXPENDITURE ON REGIONAL PREFERENTIAL ASSISTANCE
TO INDUSTRY IN ASSISTED AREAS

	Total £m			Per head £		
	1972-73	1976-77	1977-78	1972-73	1976-77	1977-78
Northern	66.0	237.0	156.0	19.1	70.3	47.2
North West	40.0	103.0	67.0	6.1	15.7	10.1
South West	5.0	12.0	9.0	5.9	14.2	11.3
Yorks. & Humber	2.0	30.0	31.0	6.4	6.5	6.6
East Midlands	0.3	2.5	2.7	0.4	3.6	4.1
English assisted areas	114.3	388.8	270.1	7.1	24.1	14.3
Scotland	85.2	216.0	145.5	16.4	41.5	28.0
Wales	53.6	113.8	91.4	19.4	41.2	32.6
All assisted areas*	254.1	719.9	507.5	10.5	29.9	21.1

*includes items which cannot be broken down below the national level.

Source: House of Commons Written Answer, 14 March, 1979. *Parliamentary Debates (Commons)* 1978-79, .208.

To criticise the 1972 U-turn is not necessarily to deny that – at least as a second-best – some degree of discretionary state investment may be necessary in present circumstances. If small firms were able to expand through retained profits, as they do in most other industrial countries; if industrial banking were as well developed as in, say, West Germany;[40] if Britain's uniquely high upper rates of income tax were reduced; there would be only a limited role for "selective assistance" and the NEB. As things are, there may be at least a transitional role for state investment or subsidy, but there is a wide range of possible systems. At one extreme is the largely commercial approach, with an arm's length relationship with the Government, which senior public sector

32

managers pray for. At the other is the pursuit of short-term employment, with little regard to longer-term costs and benefits, which some observers think was exemplified in the original "rescues" of British Leyland and Chrysler UK, or in the more recent "coups" of attracting a Hoffman la Roche factory to Scotland at a cost of £100,000 a job, or Delorean Motors to Belfast at a cost of some £50m – on the basis of predictions of sports car sales which, in the light of all previous experience, belong in the world of fantasy.

The difference between these two approaches lies in the institutional framework within which decisions are taken. If there is one lesson from the experience of public enterprise over the last hundred years, it is that the crucial distinction is not so much whether ownership is public or private, but whether the decision-makers operate in a commercial or a politically-dominated atmosphere.[41] In the 1960s, the Italian state holding company IRI (Institute per la Reconstruzione Industriale) was held up by some British economists as a model for Britain, and it influenced the creation of the Industrial Reorganisation Corporation in 1965. The problems of IRI and the Italian public sector in general are now more widely recognised.[42] They originated in the late 1950s when the Christian Democratic Party, seeing its monopoly of power beginning to be challenged by the Communist Party, extended its traditional system of small-town patronage to the state enterprises and the banking system. This led to nepotism and industrial rescues based solely on local electoral considerations. The perversion of the original unexceptional aims of the Italian state enterprises is an instructive lesson in the economics of politics, which is particularly relevant to countries which emulate Italian policy towards state enterprises without possessing the vigorous black market which gives the Italian economy an otherwise inexplicable capacity to survive and even flourish. On the other hand, there are examples of public bodies in some Continental countries (and one or two in Britain) which operate without continual political intervention, in a competitive commercial environment, and have performed well. The discussion of these questions has tended, in Britain, to be polarised between two extremes. On the one hand the more active members of the Labour Party believe in 'the dusty survival of a scheme designed to meet the problems of fifty years ago, based on a misunderstanding of what someone said a hundred years ago' as Keynes described state socialism in the 1920s.[43] On the other hand, there are those who see no role for the state in industrial affairs. In between are those who are prepared to judge by experience, and who conclude that outright nationalisation and direct political intervention in industry have been shown to have grave defects, and are prepared to consider more commercially-orientated arrangements in cases where ownership is not purely private – "BP style" financing, independence for bodies like the NEB, and greater use of decentralised bodies such as public utilities and cooperatives.

Another idea affecting the spatial economy which is perhaps worth bearing in mind for the future is that of a 'congestion tax'. This idea was put forward in the 1960s, with reference to the South-East,[44] but it seemed to me in 1973 that during massive exodus from London was not the time to introduce such a tax.[45] Nevertheless, the use of taxation rather than physical controls has attractions to those who are not sworn enemies of the price system. In retrospect, it might have been better if, beginning in the late 1940s, subsidies in the Development Areas had been accompanied by congestion taxes rather than licensing and later I.D.C's, and O.D.P's. This would have left decision-making to individual firms and avoided the defects of the political market-place. It would also have made regional policy more or less self-financing and so have prevented regional grants being held up (e.g. by Mr Tony Benn) as aids to private industry. There is also a case for using 'congestion taxes' rather than physical controls at a sub-regional level (e.g. city centres). But Britain has suffered more than any other country from the hasty and ill-considered piling-up of taxes, without adequate consideration of their aggregate effect – in both urban development and other fields.[46] Is it not time to refuse to consider any new taxes without at the same time examining which existing taxes could be reduced, simplified or abolished? When I.D.C's and O.D.P.'s have been abolished, Development Land/GainsTax simplified and reduced, all taxation indexed for inflation, and the Development Areas slimmed down, 'congestion taxes' may perhaps come into their own.

Development Agencies

In recent years there has been a growth of regional "quangos" (quasi-autonomous national government organisations) – the Welsh and Scottish Development Agencies (the counterparts to the National Enterprise Board, with some additional functions), the Development Board for Rural Wales, the Highlands and Islands Development Board, the North-East Development Council. An economic assessment of these bodies is sometimes prejudiced both by the overt arguments put forward for the creation of the N.E.B. and by a not unjustified concern about the constitutional implications of the vast number of quangos. However, the regional bodies mentioned above are considered by many people who have had experience of their work – irrespective of political affiliation – to be doing a useful job, and they deserve to be judged on what they are actually doing.

The idea that, in the field of the built environment and local industrial development, there is a role for public bodies operating partly on "enlightened commercial" principles and partly as a vehicle for subsidies is neither new nor necessarily an invitation to "creeping nationalisation". For example, Germany set up provincial development companies in 1918, to provide planning services for house construction; they have had a continuous subsequent existence and have played a useful, uncontroversial role (in construction, not ownership) in the very pluralistic and market-orientated housing system of the German Federal Republic, and are now extending their activities into urban renewal and industrial development.[47]

In spatial economic policy, the case for the *participation* of public agencies rests on the alleviation of transitional difficulties and on problems of "time horizon", as well as specifically social and cultural grounds. Take, for example the four main functions of the Welsh Development Agency: the reclamation of derelict land; the building of advance factories; the attraction of new industry; the provision of finance for, and equity participation in, small firms.

Industrial South Wales, like the North of England, bears many scars of the Industrial Revolution, which are both an eye-sore and a deterrent to new development. In some cases, it may be profitable to undertake reclamation privately and, as Sir Harold Wilson has rightly pointed out, such activity is socially beneficial;[48] in other cases it is not profitable, and some kind of agency is needed for the administration of public subsidies. In factory building, there are two extremes; at one extreme, waiting until clients are prepared to order a new factory and, at the other, building advance factories wherever a decline in employment is in prospect, with little consideration of whether they will be let, or remain let. In between, there is an intermediate field with scope for speculative building of small factories, by private and/or public bodies. Private development – according to one of the most experienced private developers – is inhibited by planning controls, which probably need to be relaxed.[49] But there is also a role for public agencies, in favourable locations where, if factories are built (and backed up by publicity, infrastructure, etc.) most of them can reasonably be expected to be let in the end. The fairly successful experience of the inter-war trading estates suggests that there is a case for such a policy in districts in which there is the prospect of a sharp decline in employment – such as towns affected by the closure of steel works. To avoid "creeping nationalisation", provisions could be incorporated for such factories to be offered for sale after a certain period. Competition between regions in publicity and salesmanship, although not without some "wastes of advertising" is probably the best guarantee that the attractions of currently "depressed" districts are not overlooked. However, independence by regional agencies – such as that displayed by the Scottish Development Agency – appears to be viewed askance in Whithall; regional agencies do not fit well into the highly centralised structure of British Government. Equity participation in small firms is partly a second best to a change in the tax system, but the Welsh Development Agency gives firms a "buy back" option which might be used if British taxation ceased to be so inimical to industrial innovation and growth.

Even under a better conceived tax system, however, there would still be a role (as in countries such as West Germany, which do have such tax systems) for public "merchant banks" operating under broadly competitive conditions but with particular responsibilities in fields where rapid sectoral or spatial economic change gives rise to special problems. This type of intervention to ease the tensions of economic change is very different from the traditional socialist pre-occupation with the virtues of state monopoly and the evils of private enterprise.

Principles in politics?

The attitude which should be taken towards the regional development agencies thus depends on the general economic and political principles being adopted. But should governments have any principles? Should they not judge every case on its merits? Recent experience suggests that this seemingly reasonable approach contains snags. Thoughtful and non-partisan critics, such as Mr Edmund Dell, have suggested that governments have attempted to do too much in industrial affairs, and lacking any basis of principle, have become embroiled in essentially managerial decisions.[50]This criticism applies to both Labour and Conservative Governments of the 1970s, despite their differences. The Labour Party traditionally prides itself on being the party of principle and intellectual doctrine, but Mr Callaghan, as Prime Minister – if not all his colleagues – represented Labour as "pragmatic" and "moderate" as against the "doctrinaire" Conservatives. Conservative politicians, on the other hand, have tended to criticise "doctrinaire socialism". There seems to be a confusion of thought here. It is "doctrinaire" to maintain a doctrine which is disproved by experience, but it is impossible to conduct a coherent policy without a set of theories, or doctrines, to explain the likely consequences of actions. Politicians who claim to be purely "pragmatic" tend to be pre-occupied with immediate tactics; when faced by unexpected developments, they are at a loss, and often seize on a currently fashionable doctrine without thinking its consequences through. Conversely, politicians committed to untenable doctrines can find in office that they have to be abandoned, leaving a doctrinal vacuum. Hence the erratic course of recent British government, in which two Labour Governments, starting with doctrinaire socialist policies, swung round in midterm to a rather incoherent pragmatism, while a Conservative Government, starting without much of an intellectual basis for policy-making, drifted into an inflationary monetary policy and then sought to suppress the consequences by adopting a somewhat doctrinaire and essentially socialist policy of price controls, pay norms and discretionary industrial subsidies. A more academic (or, rather, intellectually honest) approach by political parties would produce greater coherence in policy-making, and might well strike a responsive chord with the British electorate.

If we start, for example, from the basis of a "socially responsible market ecomony", (to translate the concept of "soziale Marktwirtschaft" which has dominated the economic policy of West Germany) this provides a touchstone to judge whether inherited institutions should be retained, abolished or modified. Ruthless surgery can be justified in some cases. For example, price control – unless it is merely a wasteful formality – is incompatible with a market economy, and in the long run can only function as part of a system based on rationing. This proposition of "positive economics" can be illustrated by efforts to control inflation by price control going back at least to the Emperor Diocletian. It is the kind of issue on which "mainstream" economists can offer a fairly agreed view of some practical value to politicians, although British academic economists can hardly have been said to have done so, since price control was introduced in 1973.

In other cases, it is a matter of balancing costs and benefits at the margin. The "job support machine", for example, which at best holds up employment temporarily, may well have been over-expanded, compared with programmes such as industrial re-training which, one would think, offer better long-term prospects of maintaining employment: the present subsidies deserve more analysis in public of the kind they appear to have received in private from the Treasury. This applies to subsidies by both central and local government. Many local authorities have begun experimenting with loans – all too easily converted into equity or grants by default – and under-priced land and factory space. This type of local competition – which has parallels in many other EEC countries – has a good and a bad side. The good side is a positive local attitude to industrial development (where it is needed) and an administrative counterweight to the previously often unsympathetic attitude to industry in many inner areas. The bad side is escalating competition for limited investment between local authorities which cannot really afford this expenditure. The beneficiaries are likely to be a mixed bag of enterprises, some of which do not need assistance, and some of which have no long-term prospects. Yet once the subsidy race begins, both local authorities and firms find it hard to stay aloof, and the system grows by its own momentum. As with international competition in subsidies, a degree of "imperfect competition" can arise which benefits no one. This danger is particularly acute when, as in the British case, most of the subsidies are paid for by the central government. It would not be unreasonable to impose some kind of limit on the extent to which the Exchequer subsidised local subsidies, leaving local authorities with the option of paying them out of local resources, or relying on appropriate planning and information policies, which are often more to the point than subsidies.

However, the current need to curb over-expanded and questionable industrial subsidies should not obscure the fact that certain types of subsidy, and certain types of action by public or semi-public agencies – notably in the regeneration of old urban districts or regions – are compatible with a market economy and can even support it, by coping with those special cases in which a market economy solves problems only at an unacceptable social cost. For example, the regional development agencies seem to me to have a useful role to play in the more variegated "regional" situation which is emerging, and one which would continue in a more market-orientated economy, with less discretionary industrial subsidy. It might, however, be possible to draw a somewhat clearer distinction between the agencies' quasi-commercial activities and investment undertaken solely on social (or political) grounds: if this were done, decisions on socially motivated subsidisation could be placed firmly with the Government, leaving the agencies free to adopt a more commercial approach.

Regional economics as development economics

I have argued in this essay that the nature of the British "regional problem" has changed, but that regional economics has not yet adjusted itself to this change.

There is a striking parallel between the reappraisal needed in regional economics and the reappraisal which has begun in development economics. Indeed, regional economics can be regarded as development economics applied to a region rather than a state. Development economics can be said to start with *The Wealth of Nations*. Adam Smith, Friedrich List and J. S. Mill stressed the importance of the social, educational and moral pre-requisites of economic development. The same points, in a modern context, were made in Sir Arthur Lewis's classic book *The Theory of Economic Growth* (1955) and his more practical *Development Planning* (1966). But the more academically fashionable and influential type of post-war "development economics" brushed such considerations aside, and emphasised the need for a 'big push' in industrial development. Many developing countries, partly as a result, made what are now accepted as serious errors in development policy. To quote Sir Arthur:

> Related to this error is the further belief that the path of economic development lies mainly through the multiplication of large-scale projects, on which attention is therefore concentrated. Plants are built on too large a scale, in anticipation of demand, so capital lies idle. Such projects employ very few people; so many countries which have high investment levels during the 1950s are now surprised to see how few new jobs have been created. These highly capital-intensive projects are very vulnerable to wage demands; since wages are a small proportion of their costs; so the ease with which they keep raising wage rates plays havoc with wages and employment in the rest of the economy.[51]

A somewhat similar outcome has occurred as a result of the establishment – after Government pressure – of car assembly plants on Merseyside. But, before embarking on any sweeping condemnation of this policy, we ought to look at the experience with similar regional development projects in other countries.

In the early 1960s it was believed that car production would expand (as indeed it did in every European country apart from the UK) and governments pressed car firms to set up new plants in "development areas". In West Germany, the government of North-Rhine-Westphalia provided incentives for car firms to set up plants in the Ruhr district, and several were started. They have operated as satisfactorily as older plants. In so far as this move would not have taken place in any event, it may be reckoned a success for state action (although in this case a type reflecting the strength of the federal structure in West Germany). But West Germany has a uniformly high standard of industrial relations and technical education, which contributes to the success of new industries. In Italy, a similar attempt was made to provide work for the South by establishing the Alfa-Romeo plant near Naples. But the Mezzogiorno is a different world from Milan – in its educational level, social attitudes and unusual (i.e. to a large extent criminally controlled) political system. In spite of modern equipment and an excellent product, the Alfa-Sud plant has experienced grave problems, which have caused the state-owned firm of Alfa-Romeo to incur massive losses.

British experience with Ford, Vauxhall and British Leyland plants on Merseyside, and the Rootes/Chrysler/Peugeot plant at Linwood, near Glasgow, has been more "Italian" than German. A study of the impact of the car plants on the Merseyside labour market shows that they did not merely "mop up" the pool of unemployment, as the prevailing theory assumed.[52] Labour was mainly poached from old industries incapable of offering such high wages. One example was the Liverpool Corporation bus service, which was permanently weakened by the haemorrhage suffered. Such denuded enterprises were henceforth unable to carry on efficiently, incapable as they were of offering the high wages which the motor industry could pay good "employable" labour. The arrival of the motor industry in effect shuffled the available hands, leaving the registered unemployed – particularly the unskilled – facing an even worse situation than hitherto, in that potential employers were increasingly hard hit by the income expectations generated locally. In short, the multiplier effect was upon wage inflation rather than the unemployed. Moreover, the productivity in some of the plants has been so low as to threaten their continued existence. One of the British Leyland Speke plants was closed in 1978, and – unless there is an improvement in performance of which there has so far been little sign – it seems unlikely that Linwood will survive.

The lesson would seem to be that regional unemployment may not be solved *merely* by setting up a car factory. It would be going too far to reject the idea of branch factories, although large plants based more on regional subsidies and official arm-twisting than on commercial calculations can sometimes be a cuckoo's egg in the sub-regional nest. The main need – as long advocated for developing countries by Sir Arthur Lewis – is for *balance*. There has to be a balance between locally based and "immigrant" firms, between large enterprises and small. Above all, job creation needs to be balanced by changes in labour's ability to respond to new job opportunities.

Structural policies in the European motor industry provide other illuminating examples of success and failure, often with regional implications. In 1960, the ailing firm of BMW was on the verge of being taken over by Mercedes-Benz. The Bavarian (regional) government, unwilling to see this famous Bavarian firm run from Stuttgart, in effect blocked this deal and helped the firm, under new management, to embark on a programme of developing sporty saloon cars, which has been so successful. Like the expansion of the car assembly in the Ruhr, this is an example of the operation of a federal system. France, on the other hand, has traditionally operated a centralised system, but a hard-headed commercial type made possible by administrators' almost complete freedom from democratic control. In 1973, the French government forced FIAT to relinquish its holding in Citroen (primarily, it would seem, on nationalistic grounds), and encouraged a step-by-step takeover by the small and provincial, but very well run, firm of Peugeot. This produced a successful organisation which was able to acquire the European assets of the fading Chrysler Corporation, thereby becoming the largest European manufacturer, and one with a potentially secure future – if it can succeed in absorbing the more indigestible parts of the Chrysler legacy.

The experience of the British motor industry has been different. In the 1950s, Britain had an efficient and successful manufacturer of commercial vehicles based in the North-West – Leyland Motors. It took over the ailing Triumph firm and looked set to become perhaps another Mercedes-Benz. Then, with Government encouragement, it took over the large group which comprised the popular manufacturers, Austin and Morris, together with the up-market firms, Jaguar, MG and Rover. The unresolved problems of Austin-Morris claimed the lion's share of the group's resources, and development was neglected of both commercial vehicles and the Jaguar/MG/Rover range, in both of which Britain's "comparative advantage" was high. This process was not changed by the state take-over in 1974. Only in 1978, very late in the day, was a more commercial type of management initiated, the success of which remains uncertain.

Can we draw any general conclusions from these and other examples of

Government intervention in industry? We can at least dispose of one common argument. This begins by listing various defects of the market system. It then concludes that the state must intervene to correct these defects, implicitly assuming that the state is operated by "philosopher-kings" solely concerned with the public good, and is free from all the imperfections of real-world market processes. This view underlies all British textbooks of regional economic theory,[53] a great deal of 'welfare economics',[54] and much British discussion of industrial policy in recent years. The Platonic view of the state implicit in this type of economic analysis tends to be regarded as naive by political scientists of the liberal, utilitarian tradition, who regard the state as an institution which responds to various pressures, and is subject to the potential failings of any human institution. A very different approach to government policy was adopted by the great political economists from Adam Smith to Arthur Lewis. To quote Sir Arthur again:

> Governments can have a notable effect on economic growth. If they do the right things, growth is advanced. If they do too little, or the wrong things or too much, growth is retarded . . . We distinguish nine ways in which governments may bring about economic stagnation or decline; by failing to maintain order, by plundering the citizens, by promoting the exploitation of one class by another, by placing obstacles in the way of foreign intercourse, by neglecting the public services, by excessive *laissez-faire*, by excessive spending and by embarking on costly wars.[44]

Recent British Governments have at least not (except in industrial relations) pursued excessive *laissez-faire* or (apart from the ill-judged "cod war" with Iceland) embarked on costly wars.

Can we say anything as to the conditions in which government intervention in industry is likely to encourage economic growth, and the conditions in which it is likely to retard it? Experience in the motor industry might suggest the hypothesis that, the more state action is influenced by trade unions, the more it will favour short-term job preservation, at the expense of long-term viability. More generally, could it be that, the more democratic the state, the more likely it is that state intervention in industry will do harm rather than good?

Regional Policy in the EEC

Regional policy – and in particular the proposed Community Regional Development Fund – attracted a great deal of attention in the EEC in the year 1972-1975, largely owing to the efforts of Mr George (now Lord) Thomson, as Commissioner for Regional Affairs. The "Thomson Strategy" placed great emphasis on the need for an active and comprehensive regional policy designed to reduce what were considered to be large and growing regional differences in the Community. This approach was summed up in the 1973 'Thomson Report',[56] which reflected the traditional economic analysis of regional economic problems which has been discussed above in a British context. The

"Thomson Strategy" was characterised by what a sympathetic American academic calls 'institutional role-playing', in which (I would suggest) both power politics and the regional economic facts tended to be overlooked.[57] Mr (now Lord) Thomson regarded the Commissioner for Regional Affairs as representing 'a Community-wide constituency of under-privileged regions'. This is a reasonable function – although some might prefer a term like 'poor' to the question-begging term 'under-privileged'. This approach was, however, "from the top down", in that international politicians and civil servants sought to do good to the 'under-privileged' regions, as opposed to the "from the bottom up" approach of giving powers to regional representatives. The Thomson Strategy was also stronger on rhetoric than analysis. Speaking of the 'moral challenge' of regional policy, Lord Thomson stated that:

> The truth is that in Europe today the under-privileged periphery is spreading. It is stretching out tentacles into the pools of poverty which are growing in the Community's prosperous heartland. (*Financial Times*, 25 July, 1975).

Perhaps, but one could equally well say that the heartland was stretching out tentacles of prosperity into the periphery. None of the statistical studies of inter-regional differences within countries has shown an unambiguous increase since the early 1960s — rather the reverse.[58] Economic differences (in incomes, unemployment, etc.) between regions *within* countries have generally narrowed. This trend began in the boom years of the 1950s and 1960s but has continued in the 1970s because of rising unemployment in the "central" regions of the EEC. On the other hand, the differences *between countries* in the EEC, after having narrowed in the 1960s, have widened in the 1970s. However, this widening (even apart from all the qualifications about the meaningfulness of national income comparisons) is attributable solely to the new members in the British Isles, and Italy; it has not applied to other members.

The "Thomson Strategy" had its heart in the right place, but at times it reminded me of the late Mr Sydney Stanley's famous words, 'Don't try to confuse me with the facts'. Professor Talbot at one point almost qualifies his enthusiasm:

> . . . a Community regional policy was one cornerstone because – it was further believed – serious economic and social inequalities existed, and would likely increase, within several sub-regions of the Community.[59] If major steps were not taken to reverse this rich-poor syndrome then it would be politically unfeasible to move towards the construction of a new Europe. Whether these inequalities were actually increasing is debatable, but the argument of increasing 'regional disparities' was politically compelling and seemed to be buttressed by a certain amount of economic commensense. (*op.cit.* p.201).

There was, and is, scope for academic debate on the nature of regional problems in the Community, and the extent to which they justify a Community policy. However, the pre-occupations of the Heath Government, which

Table XIII

INDEX OF GROSS NATIONAL PRODUCT PER HEAD AT
CURRENT PRICES & EXCHANGE RATES
(EEC average = 100)

	1970	1978
West Germany	124	141
Denmark	129	137
Belgium	107	134
Holland	99	126
Luxembourg	127	124
France	113	113
UK	89	75
Italy	70	56
Ireland	54	51

Source: Basic Statistics of the Community.

strongly supported a large Development Fund, were quite different. The British Government hoped to obtain, through the Fund, a substantial net transfer of income to the UK, thereby to a large extent offsetting the cost of the Common Agricultural Policy. ('It's a useful sum of money', as Lord Home used to say.) The argument put forward in the Thomson Report (and publicly endorsed by the British Government) was, however, purely *communitaire*. Community policy, it was argued, should be directed to evening-out regional differences in income by transfers, *via* the Community budget, from the richer to the poorer regions. Britain, it was argued, had a substantial number of poor regions: indeed, according to the Thomson Report, all British regions apart from the South-East were poorer than all other regions of the EEC outside Southern Italy. Thus the kind of regional policy required by the Community *ethos* would lead to a net gain by Britain, whereas the agricultural policy led to a net loss, but this was purely incidental. British national interest therefore coincided with the views of the Regional Affairs Directorate in Brussels, which wished to see a large-scale and comprehensive Community regional policy.

The Heath Government's approach had good points and weaknesses. It was and is, reasonable for the UK to seek to reduce the heavy net cost of the common agricultural policy as currently operated. Moreover, the approach was at least based on a coherent philosophy which could be generally accepted in the Community (an approach which France has successfully used to advance her national interests). Nevertheless, some observers had doubts from the beginning about the reliance which the UK was placing on the Regional Development Fund.[60] These doubts concerned both economic analysis and political tactics. When the agricultural policy was first established, the countries which could be expected to lose from the consequent income transfers – notably West Germany – accepted this as a price for getting the Community started. When it was merely a matter of the UK joining (or remaining in) an existing Community, Germany was less prepared to pay up, especially as the honeymoon period in the EEC was by then over. The doubters did not believe that the Regional Development Fund would go far to offset the net costs of the Common Agricultural Policy, and their doubts have so far proved only too well founded.

Table XIV

REGIONAL INCOME AS PERCENTAGE OF AVERAGE FOR AREA

	Poorest	*Richest*	*Ratio, richest/ poorest*
U.S.A. (1975)	Mississippi 60%	Alaska 175%	2.9
Australia (1973/4)	Tasmania 87%	New South Wales 105%	1.2
Canada 1973	Newfoundland 54%	Ontario 117%	2.2
W. Germany	Schleswig-Holstein 84%	Hamburg 149%	1.8
EEC (1970)* 72 regions	Calabria 41%	Paris 161%	4.0
EEC (1970)* 9 states	Ireland 57%	Belgium 123%	2.2

* At purchasing power parities.
Source: MacDougal Report.

Nor is the principle of money transfers to equalise regional income within the Community as widely accepted or as demonstrably sound as the Thomson Report and, more recently, the McDougal Report (or some statements by Commission members) imply.[61] In a federal state such as the USA, the existence of a uniform federal tax system tends to bring about income transfers from the richer to the poorer regions; specifically "regional" transfers are a small element in these transfers. (Indeed, policy can sometimes lag behind events, and operate perversely. It is alleged, at least, by spokesmen for the older industrial regions of the North-East USA, that federal policy still operates so as to transfer funds from these regions to the now more prosperous "sun belt"). However, this equalising tendency in the USA (which still leaves substantial differences) operates within a framework of broadly common institutions and policies.[62] The situation in the EEC is very different. Although there are some areas of specifically low regional income – such as Southern Italy – the main differences are between *nations* rather than regions. If Britain is relatively poor, this is because of a generally low level of income, rather than because of low incomes in certain regions. As I have argued above, regional differences in the UK (Northern Ireland being to some extent an exception) are very small. The countries with average incomes below the Community average, are the UK, Ireland and Italy (although, in the case of the UK, the figures of physical consumption suggest a substantially higher standard of living than is indicated by income figures at current exchange rates, or even price-adjusted figures). The prospective new members – Greece, Spain and Portugal – have even lower average levels of income.

It could reasonably be argued that the net effect of Community policy on the incomes of members should be either neutral or a transfer from the richer to the poorer. Under the currently rather arbitrary arrangements, the main beneficiaries *per capita* would appear to be Ireland and Denmark and the main contributors the UK and Italy. Who pays what is not, however, altogether clear (even ignoring indirect effects), mainly because of an argument as to whether MCAs (Monetary Compensation Amounts) should be attributed to the importing or exporting country. The following figures, produced for the Commission, give both calculations. They can probably be regarded as indicating the rough orders of magnitude, even if the background to their publication does not suggest that they should be treated too precisely.[63]

Of the two ways of attributing MCAs, the one giving a higher British contribution (attribution to exporting country) would appear to have more logic, if we make the reasonable assumption that, outside the Community, food imports would be obtainable at below the higher Community prices.

Even more striking is the difference between the two columns indicating the effect of Article 131 of the UK accession treaty, which limited UK contributions for five years. However the MCAs are attributed, it seems clear that, under prevailing arrangements, the UK is bound to become the largest net contributor after Article 131 lapses in 1980, if it is not so already. These figures would seem to confirm a feeling at the time that the "renegotiation" of membership in 1974/5 was far from radical.

A re-adjustment of contributions to give less perverse distribution among members may well take place in the end, after some haggling, but a major transfer of income from richer to poorer countries is a different matter. When policies and institutions vary between members as much as they do, there are likely to be limits to the readiness of the richer countries to share their wealth with the poorer. This applies particularly to any proposed payments to the UK,

Table XV

EEC NET BUDGET CONTRIBUTIONS AND RECEIPTS
BY COUNTRY IN 1978
in millions of European units of account: (1 UA equals £0.67 or $1.35)

| | Actual national balances reflecting adjustments under Article 131* | | Effect of the ending of Article 131 adjustment** |
	MCAs attributed to exporting country	MCAs attributed to importing country	
Germany	−346.8	−519.8	−133.2
France	−33.3	−321.0	−80.7
Italy	−723.4	−304.9	+50.5
Netherlands	+236.8	+57.0	−28.6
Belgium/ Luxembourg	+393.4	+350.3	−22.0
UK	−1121.6	−407.0	+302.3
Ireland	+530.5	+320.1	+12.7
Denmark	+620.4	+381.3	0

* Plus sign = net receipt; minus sign = net contribution
** Plus sign indicates a rise in contributions

Source: Commission press release, 9 April, 1979.

which is in the unique position of having been the richest country and now being among the poorer (even if not yet as poor as the national income figures suggest).

How has this reversal of fortunes occurred? It has certainly not been the result of any shortage of natural resources, compared with other EEC members. Nor is it a recent development: complaints of the effects of restrictive practices, inappropriate class attitudes and inadequate vocational training on British economic growth were made by percipient economists before 1914. There is a widespread view on the Continent that Britain is a country with every natural advantage bent on committing industrial suicide. Thus the idea that other countries should – as they see it – pay for the consequences of British folly, falls on fairly deaf ears. The stress recently laid by British representatives on the country's poverty has produced reactions nearer contempt than sympathy, (Eurojoke. 'Question: How can you recognise the plane bringing the British delegation? Answer: It is the one which, even after the engines are switched off, continues to whine').

Experience so far supports those who questioned the British policy of seeking to bring about a surreptitious gain *via* the Regional Development Fund to offset the loss caused by an unsatisfactory agricultural policy. There is still a view in the Commission and the European Parliament that the Regional Fund should be substantially expanded in order to 'balance' the expenditure on agriculture and reduce agriculture's share of the Community budget (currently about 80 per cent). But it is far from obvious that, because the Community is spending too much on agriculture it should therefore spend more on regional policy. Might it not be better simply to spend less on agriculture?[64] British governments have criticised the Common Agricultural Policy, as currently operated, for producing costly and disruptive surpluses. This is a telling criticism (if not, perhaps, one altogether consistent with talk of 'more food from our own resources') which is shared in many circles in the Community. Britain, therefore, would have potential allies if it sought to reform the Common Agricultural Policy as a member who clearly accepted Community membership and put forward coherent policies which reflected more than purely national interests. The style of diplomacy which the UK has adopted in the last few years has alienated many politicians in other member countries who are by no means unsympathetic to the changes which the British Government would like to see. On the other hand, it would be a mistake to imagine that a better atmosphere will bring any quick rewards. A clear committment to the Community need not exclude equally clear medium-term objectives for improving its functioning, pursued with diplomatic skill and a readiness to play strong national cards in pursuit of them. One can easily imagine what France would have done with North Sea oil.

Where does all this leave the Regional Development Fund? Probably playing a more modest role than either the 'Eurocrats' on philosophical grounds or the British Government on more self-interested grounds hoped to see. Even if the more ambitious ideas on 'transfer of resources' are abandoned, there is a case for channelling some Community funds to regions or districts facing particularly severe problems, both to obtain more money for them and perhaps to open them up to new ideas and influences (if direct investment by the Fund were permitted, as it is not at the moment). In 1977, the Fund paid out £246m, the lion's share going to the 'development areas' of the UK and Southern Italy. The amounts involved do little to offset the costs to Britain of the Common Agricultural Policy. The Fund seems well established, but unlikely to fulfil the high hopes originally placed on it.

Professor Talbot attributes the failure to establish as large and powerful a Regional Development Fund as originally envisaged to the oil crisis of 1973. I find this unconvincing. I would suggest that, as with other aspects of Community policy, the thinking behind the proposed regional policy lacked the wisdom of, say, *The Federalist*[65] and that this intellectual weakness, together with the fact that "regional policy" was interpreted by the British and Italian Governments as 'payments to us' had a bearing on subsequent events.

Table XVI

REGIONAL DEVELOPMENT FUND PAYMENTS, 1977.

£m

Belgium	1.9
Denmark	3.8
German Federal Republic	16.4
France	30.3
Ireland	14.6
Italy	98.8
Luxembourg	.1
Netherlands	1.9
United Kingdom	78.4
Total	246.2

Source: Regional Development Fund 1977 Report.

Professor Talbot's impressively detailed account of the origins of the Fund, and of what politicians said about it in public, contains nothing to alter my impression that there was an inadequate analytical basis to the "Thomson Strategy" and that the British Government was not concerned with regional policy at all, but with what it got out of the kitty.

Although the "Thomson Strategy" has attracted most attention, there is another aspect of Community regional policy, which reflects a different philosophy, embodied in a different branch of the Brussels secretariat. Whereas the Regional Policy Directorate-General (XVI) has been concerned with increasing the size of the Regional Development Fund, the Directorate-General for Competition (IV) has been mainly concerned with preventing an international bidding-up of regional aids. It succeeded in getting a scheme approved by the Council of Ministers in 1971 which imposed a limit of 20 per cent of the total cost of regional investment subsidies in the "more industrialised" regions of the Community. In January, 1979, this rule was renewed for three years, with an alternative limit of 3,500 European Units of Account (£2,300) per job created. However, exemptions were given for Southern Italy, Northern Ireland and the Irish Republic, where the government appears free to pay the whole cost of the investment – as Britain has often done in Northern Ireland.

Supporters of the "Thomson Strategy" have argued that the "negative" approach of limiting regional aids should be replaced by "positive" approach of the Regional Development Fund. Being less convinced that public expenditure is necessarily a "good thing", I would argue that there is a continuing need to limit the growth of the Fund, and also to reach Community agreements to limit

48

national subsidies. However, the switch from general to "selective" subsidies has largely made the existing regional limits a dead letter. Attention has therefore shifted to the possibility of some kind of Community limit on industrial subsidisation. Support for such a policy comes from West Germany, Denmark, Holland and Belgium, where there is a feeling that a massive, and to some extent internationally competitive, subsidisation of steel, ship-building, and other industries is economically harmful. This policy has been strongly resisted by the UK, France and Italy. The issue is likely to be a contentious one for some years and no effective Community regulation is likely in the immediate future. But those who question the virtues of unlimited discretionary industrial subsidisation can only hope for some kind of international "arms limitation" agreement.

Is regional economics a science?

I have suggested throughout this essay that a good deal of the regional economic analysis produced by British academics, far from illuminating current problems, has been unhelpful and misleading. If this is so, how has the situation arisen? I would put forward three possible causes: academic over-specialisation; an attempt to make the subject more "scientific" than the nature of the subject matter allows and a pre-occupation with large, and often inappropriate, aggregates.[66] For example, the idea that it is possible (in most cases) to define clear-cut economic regions is, as any geographer could have told economists, an illusion. Economic and social characteristics are sometimes sufficiently distinct to enable a reasonably clear classification of "regions". In Spain today, Catalonia, the Basque country and Andalucia are fairly distinct regions, with Andalucia having an average income about one quarter that of the other two provinces and twice the unemployment rate. But, in many cases, different regions can be drawn according to different criteria. Wales, for example, has more cultural unity than most Standard Regions but it is in no sense an economic region – rather three regions linked "horizontally" with England. Moreover, the economic differences between regions are small, and in most cases a region will score high on one criterion and low on another. East Anglia, for example, has relatively low income but does not have high unemployment or emigration.

Similarly, the distinction between "urban" and "regional" economics is unfortunate; a "macro-economic" pre-occupation with regions has blinded regional economists to what has been happening in the cities. Some textbooks have treated "urban" and "regional" economics as indivisible, but there are occupational pressures to narrow the field of study.[67] Even "urban and regional" is not altogether a satisfactory frame of reference. It is unfortunate that there has not been more development of "land economics", in the sense of the study of the economic aspects of all types of land use – urban, agricultural, forest, recreational – envisaged by Pre-War "Wisconsin School" in the USA.[68] This school had a breath of vision in its treatment of the uses to which the surface of the globe can be put, a blend of theory and practice, and an understanding of the micro-economic basis of land use which have been lacking in many recent expositions by urban or regional economists. "Models" play an indispensible role in economic studies, but it is an illusion to seek a comprehensive model which will provide an analogue for the spatial economy as accurate and operational as, say, an engineer's calculation of stresses in a bridge (and any user of the Severn Bridge must conclude that it is not easy to do it for bridges, either). Economics can, however, be scientific in the more fundamental sense that it is based on honesty in the use of facts and arguments; an understanding of a few basic concepts of scientific method, such as the nature of casual hypotheses and the inadmissibility of extrapolating recent trends indefinitely into the future; a search for the widest possible range of data, which means historical and international comparisons; and a reasoned examination of all points of view. In addition, what is surely needed in the study of spatial economic problems is more dialogue between economists, geographers, sociologists, industrial managers, surveyors, town planners and other specialists, and an attempt to distil conclusions relevant to current problems. Whether the academic reward-system encourages this type of approach is a different question. Are there perhaps more academic rewards in making simple matters appear complicated than in bringing out the often essentially simple issues underlying complex phenomena?

An innovation-based regional policy?

'Traditional' regional policy has not been confined to the UK, nor has it begun to be questioned only in the UK.[69] In most "developed" countries, policy in the 1950s and 1960s was concerned to move industry from "congested" to "under-developed" regions. In all these countries – although in varying degrees – the 1970s have seen a change in the economic climate, with lower growth, lower investment and higher unemployment; economists in several countries have begun to question whether, in this changed economic climate, traditional regional policy is still relevant, and have begun to suggest alternatives. (On the other hand, the "traditional" school, which is particularly strong in Great Britain, has suggested that in these conditions – and especially if the UK remains in the EEC – "regional policy" may need to be "strengthened"). At the same time, some students of the social consequences of science have begun to argue that the silicon chip will have more far-reaching effects on the economy, probably with regional implications, than most economists and administrators yet realise. I should like to discuss briefly some ideas put forward in West Germany and the USA, as well as Great Britain, which all point towards alternatives to traditional regional policy.

The study of regional economics in West Germany has tended to have a broader scope than in Great Britain, with more emphasis on the analysis of the district against the region, and the importance – in the traditionally decentralised German system – of provincial and local political action.[70] Even more radical and illuminating ideas arise from some research by business economists at the International Institute of Management, Berlin.[71] This research consists of (a) case-studies of firms' investment decisions and the factors influencing them; (b) studies of the reasons why some firms and some districts are more successful in innovating new products than others. This school of research pays particular attention to the dynamic aspects of economic life deriving from the Austrian School, and the importance of power relationships and the influence of technology on organisations which – to non-Marxists – are the most enduring legacies of Marx.

The traditional school of regional economics tends to follow neo-Keynesianism in dealing in aggregates such as "investment", "output", or "employment" which, it is assumed, can be diverted from regions where there is too much to regions where there is too little. However, "output" is made up of a variety of products which are constantly being born, expanding and then contracting: moreover, production relationships are always changing but are periodically subject to dramatic changes resulting from new technology. Thus output and employment in a region depend partly on locational factors – which can be influenced by changes in transport facilities. But of increasing importance is the ability to innovate new or improved products and successfully carry out the production sequence of design, manufacture and marketing. In the "developed" countries this is coming to depend less on the quantity and price of inputs than on their *quality*, in the sense of the skills and attributes needed for good design, harmonious production, effective marketing. Whereas the traditional view of regional policy tends to regard technology and skill as exogenous or "given", the "Berlin school" argues that their level and spatial distribution depend to a large extent on organisational structure, in both public administration and industry. There has been a tendency to concentrate "headquarter functions" in metropolitan districts. In mono-centric countries such as the UK and France, this concentration has occurred in the national capital: in a poly-centric country like the German Federal Republic it has occurred in provincial capitals and other cities of around a million inhabitants. In so far as these cities possess "agglomeration economies", it is because it is easy to arrange face-to-face contacts with important decision-makers or consultants (which are likely to remain important, in spite of electronics); because research material, trade exhibitions, etc., are concentrated there, and services of all sorts are available.

This view of regional development has led the Berlin economists to a view of regional policy based on building up the capability of some "development areas" to innovate new products by raising the quality of their resources, rather than trying to divert production of established products from metropolitan areas. The traditional "diversion" approach suffers from the defect that the established production which can be diverted is likely to be towards the top of the 'growth and decline curve'. If a large firm producing a standard product is induced to set up branch factories in a development area (often eliminating local firms, by direct takeover, or by attracting labour from them), it may before long experience a fall in demand for the product. The development area could then be in a worse situation than if it had relied more on local entrepreneurship. (There is also the possibility, especially under a system of grants as compared with tax allowances, of attracting "subsidy mongers" whose aim is to make a quick killing. But there is no evidence that this has occurred on a significant scale).

The Berlin economists have put forward several suggestions for modifying the regional policy of the German Federal Republic. The following are three of their suggestions, which *mutatis mutandis* apply to other countries as well:

(a) Government policies should be examined for unintended regional biases. For example, policies which work down through administrative hierarchies tend to lose their impetus as they go down the line. Thus government policies for encouraging research, or providing venture capital, have tended to favour the more successful firms in the more successful areas. The answer is, on the one hand, to decentralise the provision of these government aids and, on the other hand, to encourage 'horizontal' rather than 'vertical' linkages. (The linkages between the co-operative banks and the non-profit housing enterprises which have contributed to giving them an important role in the West German banking and housing sectors could presumably be cited as examples.) In Great Britain, perhaps one of the most effective aids to horizontal linkages would be a reliable telephone system.

(b) Competition policy should be viewed in the light of its long-run regional effects. For example, mergers can sometimes lead to a movement of 'headquarter functions' to other districts. This does not show up in economic statistics, but could have important long-run consequences.

(c) The size and number of development areas has to be limited, if efforts to achieve more activity in them are to be successful. There are at present 320 'development centres' in the German Federal Republic: these could be reduced to about 60.

These and similar ideas have been put forward with reference to West Germany, which believes itself to have regional problems, although to an outside observer they would seem to be small ones. The West German economy also suggests two points of particular relevance to the United Kingdom. Firstly, the long established devolution of political power to provinces and communities has had the effect of decentralising the supply of managerial skills, cultural facilities and many other 'intangibles' which have important long-run effects on the regional distribution of economic activity. Secondly, casual empiricism suggests that bread, beer or sausages are more likely to be produced by local firms than in the UK. This ties up with the statistical evidence that there are more small firms in such industries in West Germany than in the United Kingdom.[72] There is a *prima facie* case that this difference is related to the more favourable tax treatment of small businesses in West Germany.

An impressively detailed 'micro-economic' study has been undertaken for the USA by the Massachussetts Institute of Technology[73]; it covered no less than 5.6m firms over the period 1960-1976. The most striking finding was the high rate at which firms were born and grew, but also declined and died. Changes in employment are the small differences between the two large figures of jobs created and jobs lost. The creation of new jobs took place mainly in small firms: between 1960 and 1976, 66 per cent of new jobs created were in firms of less than twenty employees. The author concludes that, for both national and regional employment policy (in the USA), the emphasis should be neither on dealings with large firms which create little new employment, nor on an attempt to delay firm deaths ('job preservation') but on the environment which influences job creation in small firms. (It should be added that, towards the end of the survey period, and subsequently, this environment became much less favourable for small firms, through changes in tax arrangements and the capital market and the growth of regulatory agencies, which by their nature seem to favour large firms.)

The view of the job creation process which emerges from these German and American studies is *mutatis mutandis* applicable to the UK, and is a more 'biological' one than that which has underlain traditional regional policy – a continual cycle of birth, growth, maturity and decline, for both firms and products. The government has an important role to play in this process, but mainly by affecting the environment in which birth and growth occurs. A parallel can be drawn with gardening. A gardener can remove obstacles to plant growth by improving soil nutrients or combating pests but, whatever he does, some plants will do well in some parts of the garden and not in others. A policy on regional (and neighbourhood) economic change which envisages the Government's role as that of a gardener is in some ways more intellectually and administratively demanding than one which envisages the Government's role as that of God. It is easy to draw up a plan for so many car plants or steel works

53

to be set up in development areas, (or, on a neighbourhood level, to condemn an area of 19th century housing and bulldoze it in preparation for council redevelopment). It is more difficult to find out the constraints on the growth of business, and implement programmes to reduce them, or to find out the needs and aspirations of residents and businessmen in a neighbourhood and implement a plan which permits gradual, 'cellular' renewal.[74] A government which does not believe in the traditional forms of 'intervention' is not thereby freed from the need to undertake surveys and devise plans: in some ways, both surveys and plans have to be more intricate and subtle.

The silicon chip and the regional economy[75]

The effect of technological change in general, and micro-processing in particular, on the regional distribution of economic activity, has been neglected by regional economists. This is one of the issues which should be examined in a wider approach to regional policy.

The discussion of the 'silicon chip revolution' has tended to be polarised between two extremes. The pessimists adopt a crude labour-displacement theory, implicitly assuming that there is a fixed amount of work to be done, and ignoring the 'income effects' of labour-saving technology. The optimists argue that technical innovations have been successfully absorbed since the Industial Revolution, and that the micro-processor is no different. It may be granted that the micro-processor is *in principle* no different from the power loom or steam engine – although it is worth bearing in mind that they, in their time, caused considerable regional change and dislocation. But the extent of the cost saving made possible by the micro-processor – several thousand times compared with previous systems – puts it in a different class from most previous inventions. It promises social gains through the elimination of repetitive and boring work, but it is also bound to raise serious social problems through the displacement of traditional skills. The effects are likely to be different in different types of industry, and this could have regional implications.

The main requirements for the actual manufacturing of silicon chips is a supply of highly skilled scientists, and this activity is tending to settle in districts where research institutions are situated, and where scientists are prepared to live, e.g. California. The siting of the Inmos micro-chip project is illuminating. The (Labour) Government wanted it to go to a Development Area but the directors maintained that staff could not be attracted to such places, and chose Bristol for the headquarters. When the second instalment of capital became due, however, the (Conservative) Government was able to insist that the factory be situated at Cardiff – only half an hour away and not notably poorer in amenities than Bristol. The scope for influencing the siting of science-based industries appears to be severely limited by the environment. For the older industrial areas, environmental tidying-up and the provision of high-class leisure activities are not luxuries, but can be important elements in their economic future.

The second group consists of traditional industries, the future of which is threatened by the silicon chip. An example is the Swiss watch industry. By going over to electronic movements just in time, the Swiss industry has probably ensured its survival, but there may well be other industries which will be less fortunate, and plant closures can often have serious effects on a local labour market.

The third group of industries are those which are unlikely to be eliminated or shifted *en masse* but in which micro-processing will play an important role, e.g. automatic control in car manufacture. Firms which lag seriously behind in the introduction of these techniques are likely to become uncompetitive, and risk succumbing to competition from firms which have introduced them, possibly in other countries, except in so far as a country is willing and able to adopt a 'Burmese solution'.

The fourth group contains service industries, in some of which (e.g. as banking has already shown) there is extensive scope for the use of electronics. The long-run spatial consequences could take two contradictory forms. On the one hand, computers linked by phone can allow greater de-centralisation of facilities. On the other hand, computerisation can serve as a means of centralising control. The degree of administrative centralisation prevailing when electronic systems are introduced is therefore crucial. If the administrative system – in government or industry – is already centralised, the power of the centre is likely to be increased. Thus devolution takes on a new importance – although in the British case the autonomy of local government has been so undermined, and regional devolution so delayed, that it may now be difficult to resist the centralising tendencies. Centralisation of this type presents not only political dangers: it is also extremely vulnerable to breakdowns or sabotage.

The silicon chip revolution thus illustrates the theme of this essay – the influence of technical change, social attitudes, educational levels and political organisation on the spatial economy, and the need to take account of these influences in framing government policies. Minimising the social costs of the silicon chip requires honest discussions at every level from managing director to office boy; this is easier said than done, but there are some examples. In the 'post industrial' era which seems to be dawning there will still be a need for a regional policy of a kind but, to cope effectively with the problems of that era, it will have to be of a different kind from the traditional policy of the post-war period.

Devolution

The question of the devolution of power to regional authorities, and its possible economic consequences, is a large one, which concerns not only Great Britain but also other European countries such as Spain and France in which some regions are reacting against centralised government. Although distinct from 'regional policy' in the usual sense, it is probably of more fundamental importance. Space permits only three general points.[76] Firstly, a federal system – or a system of extensive provincial devolution – is possible. Experience, not only in large countries like Canada but also in small countries like West Germany, or even Italy, makes it quite clear that such a system does not necessarily mean the break-up of a nation, or economic ruin. One can argue for breaking away from an existing nation state, as the Irish Republic has done, and as some Scottish and Welsh nationalists would like to do. Alternatively, one can argue for a centralised system, such as the current British one, or for various degrees of devolution or federalism. (The distinction between 'devolution', in any meaningful sense, and 'federation' of the West German or Swiss kind is more semantic than real.) The point which ought to be recognised by all parties is that there is a spectrum of possible systems within a nation state.

Secondly, the only intellectually coherent system – and probably the only satisfactory system in the long run – is a symmetrical one for the whole country. Such a system was put forward by the academic members of the Kilbrandon Commission, involved regional governments not only for Scotland and Wales, but also for English regions.[77] To propose a fair amount of devolution for Scotland and Wales, while maintaining that any regional devolution in England would 'damage the structure of the United Kingdom' was far from convincing.[78]

Thirdly, the intellectual argument on 'devolution' versus 'centralism' cannot overlook local government. If the aim is to bring decision-making nearer ordinary people, this logically implies the maximum feasible devolution to the lowest tier of government. Virtually all countries with powerful provincial governments also have powerful local authorities, while countries like Sweden or Denmark do not have provincial governments, but do have far more powerful local authorities than the UK, with extensive independent sources of finance. Great Britain, in the 1974 reorganisation, has created the largest local authorities in Europe, purportedly with the aim of making them more effective governing bodies. However, their power has, in fact, been steadily reduced. Functions such as health and water have taken away from them, while the current financing system – under which the limitations of local rates forces reliance on a range of discretionary grounds and a rate support grant which is so complicated that no one outside Whitehall understands how it works – is ideally suited to transferring power from local authorities to Whitehall (which could explain why the recommendations of the Layfield Committee have been ignored).[79] The undermining of the power of local authorities has gone so far in Great Britain that several writers have seriously suggested that they should be abolished. This is a strange background to 'devolution'.

In the light of these principles, what can one say about the proposals which were put to Welsh and Scottish voters on 1 March 1979? Anyone who favours administrative and political devolution, without being a regional nationalist, must have had mixed feelings. The need for devolution can be an aspect of a 'liberal utilitarian' philosophy which seeks to meet the demands of individuals and small groups by favouring a market system as against government action, where this is possible, and, where it is not, devolving as much government action as possible to the lowest tiers of government, so that it is responsive to local demands. West Germany provides a good example of such a system. On the other hand, regional nationalism can be – and in the past hundred years in Europe generally has been – motivated by profoundly anti-liberal principles. A regional government for Scotland or Wales combined with weak local authorities, a 'first past the post' franchise and an absence of legal control on government might ultimately reproduce all those features of British central government which have been the subject of radical criticism by, among others, the Liberal Party and Lord Hailsham.[80] 'A Socialist Wales for ever' was one of the attractions of the Wales Act held out by one 'pro-devolutionist' Labour MP. Such a prospect has little appeal even to those who. like the author, would welcome a system on West German lines for Great Britain.

Nevertheless, there is, I would argue, an overwhelming case for a more decentralised system of government in the UK, in which some kind of regional level is necessary. To anyone who favours such a system, the 'devolution' episode of the 1970s has been a tragically wasted opportunity. It started off on the wrong foot with the majority report of the Kilbrandon Commission, which was pre-occupied with what it considered to be the special problems of Wales and Scotland, and so unintentionally encouraged the view that devolution meant 'the break-up of the United Kingdom'. Then came the 1974 reorganisation of local government (undertaken with no reference to regional government) which was widely, and justifiably, regarded as having done little more than increase costs and bureaucracy, and provided the worst possible background to proposals for new assemblies. Then – on a constitutional issue which pre-eminently called for a bi-partisan approach – the Labour Government acted independently, largely on the basis of short-term electoral calculations, and the Conservative Party responded in kind. The preparation of the legislation was, in consequence, conducted in unseemly haste (many of the clauses of the Scotland and Wales Bills were not even discussed in Parliament) and the level of debate in the devolution campaign plumbed depths which even exceeded those of previous 'great debates'. After the referenda and the Conservative election victory, it remains to be seen what alternative, if any, will be produced by the new Government. A non-Welsh academic observer (who, in spite of grave reservations, voted 'Yes' for the Wales Act, as a move towards de-centralisation) can only stress the continuing need for a coherent approach to the functions, financing and legal control of *all* tiers of government *throughout the United Kingdom* – an approach which was singularly lacking in the 'devolution' proposals of the 1970s.

Conclusions

There is a recurrent tendency in economics for important new ideas to ossify into a dogma, which lacks the breadth of vision of the original ideas, fails to re-interpret unchanging objectives in the light of changing conditions, and possesses less and less relevance to current problems. Economists from Adam Smith to Keynes have suffered in this way. Something of this sort seems to have happened to regional economics in Britain. The slump of the 1930s highlighted the problems of certain older industrial areas which were dangerously dependent on a few heavy industries. The Barlow Report of 1940 drew attention to the problems of these areas, and to the problems of congestion in some big cities; it reflected a widespread feeling that measures should be taken to assist the development of new industries in South Wales, Tyneside, Clydeside, etc. The policy which emerged was based on what may be termed the 'black and white' view of the British economy. The 'black' areas on the map were those in which there was allegedly too little employment, together with low incomes and poor infra-structure; and 'white' areas were those in which there was allegedly too much employment. A shift of industrial investment from 'black' to 'white' areas was to be encouraged by subsidies and licensing. Over the years, the black area has been extended until in 1978 it covered two-thirds of the UK.

In the early post-war years there was considerable justification for the 'black and white' view, and for the policies adopted, even though both black and white areas covered districts with very different economic conditions. Over time, however, this view of the problem began to diverge more and more from reality. Regional differences in unemployment rates and average incomes fell to levels which were either unimportant or not susceptible to government policy directed at investment: migration flows between regions were sometimes in the 'wrong' direction. At the present time, economic differences *within* regions are far larger than differences *between* regions, some of the most important problems at the moment being in inner-city areas, which are sometimes in development areas, sometimes not; moreover, those in development areas have not been helped much by 'regional policy'.

Instead of pointing out in good time the changing nature of spatial economic problems, British regional economists of the 'macro-economic' or 'neo-Keynesian' school have developed complex models still based on the 'black and white' view. Moreover, the attempt to make theories purely economic – excluding the social, cultural and strategic considerations which influenced the Barlow Commission – has made them even less realistic. The superficial precision of the 'macro-economic' estimates of the number of jobs created by regional policy conceals many questionable assumptions. The 'macro-economic school – with its emphasis on 'regions' which often have little economic basis – has tended to distract attention from the fact that Britain's problems are primarily national rather than regional and that, in so far as these problems are spatial, they involve *districts* (rather than regions) with a range of social and physical problems ignored in the 'macro-economic' calculus. Journalists, administrators, geographers and politicians have generally perceived these changes sooner than the regional economists.

The decline in regional differences in Great Britain has been followed by a decline in regional assistance from a high point in 1966-70. In itself, this might be considered a rational adjustment to changing circumstances. What is disturbing is the extent to which the 'black and white' policy has been replaced by 'selective' aid, without adequate examination of the issues involved. To argue that the case against discretionary industrial subsidies should be examined – instead of being dismissed on the grounds that this view is 'simplistic' or 'callous' – is not to say that the critical view has to be accepted *in toto*. A temporary subsidy may be a necessary accompaniment of an industrial restructuring – although it can also be a substitute for it. But a subsidy linked to clear-cut structural changes, and reduced as they come into effect, is very different from the kind of policy which has mushroomed since 1972, and which appears to have the objective of short-term job preservation rather than any longer-term structural aim.

Other developed countries have also pursued the 'traditional' type of regional policy based on a movement of established industry to 'development areas', and in these countries the 'traditional' policy is also being called in question. In a situation where parts of the 'non-assisted areas' have more serious problems than parts of the 'assisted areas', and in a climate of lower economic growth, it is being questioned whether it is possible or desirable to pursue the 'traditional' policy. Business economists, urban geographers and land economists in several countries have independently developed ideas for an alternative regional policy based on removing the physical and social obstacles to economic activity in certain regions or districts, rather than diverting established industry to them. This alternative view links up with older economic traditions than neo-Keynesian regional economics, and with a parallel reassessment of the nature of economic growth which is beginning in 'development economics'.

As far as British regional subsidies are concerned, the situation now seems to call for a slow and steady change of emphasis, rather than any dramatic change. (There have been too many dramatic changes in the details of British regional policy.) With the abolition of the Regional Employment Premium in 1976, the amount of assistance to the assisted areas has been substantially reduced, and a period of relative stability in regional grants seems appropriate. The assisted areas are at present (Spring 1979) almost certainly too large. On the 'alternative view' of regional policy, the longer term aim should be to concentrate regional aid on districts anywhere in the country facing particularly serious problems of spatial adjustment, while at the same time, paying more attention to the institutional factors (including unintended biases in national policy) which affect local economic growth. The process can, however, be a gradual one, and certainly will be, given the inevitable resistance to any removal of 'assisted area' status.

The fact that British 'regional policy' in the traditional sense is slowly disappearing, like the Cheshire Cat in 'Alice in Wonderland', does not mean there will not, in the future, be regional issues. Indeed, there is every indication that, Britain, as in several other highly centralised EEC countries, the question of regional autonomy will be a more contentious one than in the post-war era. Nor does it mean that there will not be spatial economic problems, although they are likely to concern *districts* rather than regions. A great deal of attention is now being devoted to the problem of the 'inner city': this concern is welcome, even if it has come twenty years too late. But incipient problems in the districts should not be overlooked – the suburban council estates, perhaps. Nor should the countryside be forgotten. Problems of rural transport and village schools have recently attracted attention, but the underlying question concerns employment in the countryside and policies towards light industry, forestry, recreation, etc. Moreover, the growth of electronic technology is likely to have considerable economic effects, with possible regional consequences. Regional development agencies seem likely to have a continuing role in dealing with these new problems.

Regional policy in the EEC is unlikely to be of major importance, even though significant amounts of public investment money are being, and are likely to continue to be, channelled through the Regional Development Fund. Most of the discussion of 'regional policy' in the EEC has not in fact been concerned with regional issues at all, but with monetary transfers between nations. The British Government has attempted to obtain net benefits from the Regional Development Fund to offset the net costs of the Common Agricultural Policy. Italy and Ireland have also argued their claims. There is likely to be further international horse-trading of this type, but it seems clear that the attempt to use regional policy as a means of offsetting the international transfers arising from an unsatisfactory agricultural policy has failed. The issues of agricultural policy and the EEC budget will have to be tackled directly.

The phase of British regional policy which began with the Barlow Report seems to have run its course. In the future, regional problems in Britain will be more concerned with the problems of political power which have tended to be glossed over in recent years, and with the elimination of environmental and human handicaps in certain areas, which will be 'sub-regional' rather than regional. There will still be problems and policies of a geographical kind, but they will be different from 'the regional problem' and 'regional policy' in the sense these terms have acquired since the War.

POSTSCRIPT

This essay was written in late 1978 and early 1979. Since then, there has been a change of Government. It seems worth reviewing the latest developments in four fields discussed above: the assisted area map, office location policy, the NEB, and the British budgetary contribution in the EEC. The Conservative Secretary of State for Industry, Sir Keith Joseph, after a two-month Departmental review, announced changes in regional subsidies (July 17, 1979). The main change is a reduction in the size of the assisted areas – although some areas will be upgraded, and a few new assisted areas created . The aim is, over a three year transitional period, to reduce the total size of the assisted areas so that the employed population in them falls from 50 per cent to 25 per cent of the employed UK population, and to concentrate assistance on 'the areas with the most intractable problems of employment'. The three-fold division of Special Development Areas, Development Areas and Intermediate Areas is retained, and the situation in Northern Ireland remains unaltered. These changes amount, broadly speaking, to rolling back the Assisted Areas map to something mid-way between the map of the early and the late 1960s.

• Development grants in the Development Areas are to be reduced from 20 to 15 per cent, and abolished in the Intermediate Areas, thus increasing the differential in favour of the Special Development Areas. Selective aid under the Industry Act will be severely curtailed in non-assisted areas; in assisted areas, it will be applied more selectively, with the aim of limiting it to projects which would not otherwise have been undertaken. (Since then, the major items of selective aid have been approved. The NEB has been authorised to build a titanium plant at Shotton, using a process favoured by Rolls-Royce which is being abandoned by ICI and is used in no other country. And some £23 million s being paid to the Dow Corning Company to expand its production of silicones in South Wales, employing 125 extra men.) On government factories, Sir Keith stated that "We consider that factory building is a useful and relatively inexpensive instrument of regional industrial policy, and this will continue. We intend, however, to secure a greater element of self-financing".

Table XVII

PROPOSED CHANGES IN REGIONAL DEVELOPMENT GRANTS
(1976 rates: proposed rates after 1982 in brackets)

		Special Development Areas	Development Areas	Intermediate Areas
		%	%	%
(I)	Buildings	22 (22)	20 (15)	20 (Nil)
(II)	Plant and machinery	22 (22)	20 (15)	Nil (Nil)

The regional development agencies in Wales and Scotland are to remain, with some reductions in their budgets, but the Regional Economic Planning Councils in England will be wound up. The exemption limit for which an Industrial Development Certificate is needed (in non-assisted areas) is raised to 50,000 square feet, thus removing most schemes from this control.

It is estimated by the Government that the proposed changes will eventually reduce expenditure on regional investment subsidies by £233m, about one-third of the previously planned expenditure. (However, since the payments in the upgraded areas will start at once, while the reduction in payments elsewhere will take place later, the immediate effect on expenditure will be small.) Government spokesmen have stated that, on the best departmental calculations, the changes will have no net effect on the number of jobs; Labour Party/trade union critics have cited calculations of a loss of 80,000 jobs.

As I have been mainly concerned in this essay, not to advocate a specific programme, but to set regional policy in a broader economic and political context, question the foundations of 'macro-economic' regional calculations, and stress the considerable changes in the spatial economy of the UK since the 'traditional' policy was introduced, I shall not discuss the proposed changes in detail (or amend what I have already written). I have suggested above that, as a long-term aim, a reduction in the size of the assisted areas would be appropriate in the new situation; the proposed changes appear to be based on this kind of thinking, and should, on the whole, be welcomed.

However, two qualifications have to be made. In the first place, the changes are somewhat negative in character; the regional subsidy changes may not do much harm, but they will equally not do much good for Britain's decaying industrial cities. Anyone who believes that the main problems of 'the areas of intractably high unemployment' (Clydeside, Merseyside, etc.), lie in a discouraging social and physical environment must wonder whether the continued policy of relying on high subsidies on industrial investment is sufficient, and hope that these regional changes will later be accompanied by a well conceived statement of policy on 'inner city' problems – and that such a policy will be implemented over more than the life-span of one government. Similarly, the widening up of the English Regional Economic Planning Councils leaves unaltered the essentially unsatisfactory nature of regional administration in England. The criticism has long been made that the Councils have been mere 'talking shops', with no direct link with administration. Regional administrations exist in England (for health, water, etc.), but they are independent of each other, often cover different areas, and are something of a law unto themselves. Few would mourn the passing of the Regional Economic Planning Councils if they were to be replaced by a more effective system of regional administration, even without elected political representatives. As it is, the whole question of 'regionalism' in England – as well as Scotland, Wales and Northen Ireland – remains open.

The second worrying aspect is that these proposals, in themselves so modest and defensible, have aroused furious opposition in the Labour Party – a not unfamiliar type of situation. One can only wish that the ground had been better prepared for the changes; 'revisionist' ideas on regional policy are only now beginning to be seriously considered by British economists.[1] The episode illustrates once again the effects of the institutionalised discouragement of radical, informed, open and early discussion of social and economic change, to which I have drawn attention above.

There have, secondly, been changes in office location policy embracing the ending of Office Development Permits; the scaling-down of the policy of civil service dispersal from a further 25,000 to 7,000; the winding up of the Location of Offices Bureau. Most people with practical experience hold that ODPs (and IDCs) have had far more effect in discouraging investment than in displacing it: on this basis, the change must be wholeheartedly welcomed. The reduction of civil service dispersal has aroused different reactions, cutting across some established lines. It was quietly welcomed by all but one of the civil service unions, which had opposed the Labour Government's policy. However, the deputy secretary of the Civil and Public Services Association attacked the new policy as 'an unparalleled example of economic lunacy and regional vindictiveness' which would cost the economy £320m. As against this, Lord Soames, Lord President of the Council, argued that it was economically sensible, because of the evening-out of London and provincial office rents, and would save £200m of public expenditure over five years. It is difficult to be definite on this question – except that the decision is certainly not paralleled economic lunacy. Even on a critical view of this decision – involving only 18,000 jobs – one can easily think of a dozen others in British post-war economic history which were incomparably more lunatic. The background is that the previous Government had subordinated efficiency to 'regional policy'. A report by Sir Henry Hardman, in 1973, had distinguished between an 'efficient solution', which would provide civil service functions at the lowest cost, and a 'regional solution', which would direct them to assisted areas with the highest unemployment rates. He recommended an intermediate course, but the Labour Government in effect adopted the 'regional solution'. In these circumstances, there seems to be a case for pausing for reflection on the policy of dispersal *with unchanged civil service functions*. The more fundamental question concerns 'devolution'; a devolution of functions would inevitably mean a dispersal of certain categories of personnel."

The Location of Offices Bureau fell victim to a review of 'Quangos', on the grounds that there was no longer a need to disperse office employment from London. However, there is evidence that the Bureau provided useful independent information to both firms moving within the UK, and international firms considering a move to the UK, which was not otherwise readily available and which these firms might well have been prepared to pay for. It has recently been claimed, with some justice, that some Labour local authorities have cut useful services, such as nursery schools or evening classes, instead of making charges (or higher charges) for them, because of either a socialist prejudice against the price mechanism or a desire to embarrass the Government. But the same argument applies to a service like that of the LOB; its original *rationale* had undoubtedly gone, but it had showed signs of adapting itself to new functions, and an experiment in reducing public expenditure by imposing user charges might perhaps have been tried.

Thirdly, there is the question of Conservative policy towards the National Enterprise Board. After the Secretary of State's initial statement in July, 1979, it seemed that a 'middle way', acceptable to the existing Board, had been found. The NEB was to remain, but with a different emphasis; its function was not to extend public enterprise but to manage the 'lame ducks', develop some high-technology (especially computer) projects, aid small firms, and act as a development agency for the North and North-West of England. It would be encouraged to sell off enterprises as soon as they became profitable. The Chairman of the NEB, Sir Leslie Murphy, said "I think that this is a very sensible compromise".

But this acceptance by the Board of the new course was abruptly ended by the Government's decision (to be implemented in a forthcoming Industry Bill) to remove Rolls-Royce (1971) Ltd., from the NEB's supervision. On being informed of this decision, the entire board resigned (November 1979), and the new board contained no trade union members. (The Chairman of the TUC doubted whether any self-respecting trade unionist would be prepared to serve, although places on the Board have been left for trade union members.) The background was a feud which had been running for two years between the Chairman of Rolls-Royce, Sir Kenneth Keith, and the NEB. The NEB was critical of what it considered to be the company's loose cost control and wishful thinking in financial planning. When the Rolls-Royce Board refused to accept its suggestions, the NEB reportedly asked the Labour Government to dismiss Sir Kenneth, hoping to change the management of Rolls-Royce in the same way as it had changed the management of BL with the appointment of Sir Michael Edwardes. Sir Kenneth counter-attacked with a vigorous campaign to remove Rolls-Royce from the control of 'this bureaucratic contraceptive'. Senior civil servants, occupationally suspicious of independent bodies like the NEB, sided with Sir Kenneth. The incoming Secretary of State for Industry, after being subjected to conflicting pressures for some months, decided against the NEB. His argument was that there were too many layers of supervision of state-owned enterprise and that the company board of directors should be left to get on with the job, without being 'second guessed' by another board.

Two questions arise. On the specific issue of Rolls-Royce (and probably BL), the question is: on past experience, will the more commercial approach desired by the Government be more likely to be achieved when supervision is carried out by the Department of Industry rather than by a semi-independent board mainly composed of businessmen? (The NEB, incidentally, exercised a similar function to the Supervisory Board which is universal in West German industry, both public and private. And as far as 'bureaucracy' is concerned, one may reasonably doubt whether the extra staff employed by the Department of Industry will be less than the number employed by the NEB to monitor Rolls-Royce, which was two.) The more general question concerns the effect on the policies of a possible future Labour Government. The affront to the inherited Board has been deplored in the Labour Party, and welcomed in the Conservative Party, as 'NEB bashing'. One cannot help recalling what happened after a Conservative Government abolished the Industrial Reorganisation Commission in 1970 (or the even longer-running see-saw in urban land policy[11]). Many moderate men in all political parties, or none, are conscious of the defects of comprehensive nationalisation and political control of industry. Although accepting the need, in some cases, for state intervention, they would like public shareholding to be subject to a stable, professional, largely market-orientated, management system. The desirability of such a system is a theme in most of the academic literature on public enterprise over the last decade. Has the Rolls-Royce decision, and the consequent clean sweep of the Labour-appointed board, made it more, or less, likely that, in the long run, such a system will be implemented and maintained? Time will tell. In the immediate future, however, there is no reason why the NEB should not continue with the other functions outlined by the incoming Government ('catalytic' investment in conjunction with private institutions, aid to small firms, regional development); this is still a very sensible compromise[III].

Finally, there is the issue of British contributions to the EEC. At the 1979 summit meeting in Dublin, Mrs Thatcher demanded financial rebates to give 'rough balance' in financial transactions with the Community. The other members offered a cut of £340m per annum through the 'corrective mechanism' devised in 1975. Mrs Thatcher rejected this 'one-third of a loaf'. At the Luxembourg summit in April, 1980, she was offered 'two-thirds of a loaf' which she again rejected. But at the end of May, after protracted negotiation, the British Government was offered slightly better terms, which it accepted. The agreement provides that the estimated net contributions of £1.08 billion for 1980 will be cut to £371m and a ceiling of £455m placed on net contributions for 1981 and 1982. These concessions must be considered a considerable success for Mrs Thatcher's toughness in negotiation, but the price for them was the virtual abandonment of the Commission's proposals to deal with the mounting cost of the Common Agricultural Policy, which constitutes the main problem for Britain. The problem of Britain's contributions has merely been postponed for two years, and will re-emerge at a time when the Community faces the problem of the cost of the agricultural policy outrunning the available financial resources. These problems could once more threaten the coherence of the Community, especially if the Labour Party is virtually committed to British withdrawal. The alternative – as the German Chancellor has urged – is for the Community to tackle the cost of the agricultural policy more effectively and to devise some general system of financing which is accepted as reasonably equitable by all members. This point was made, before Dublin, in Professor Ralf Dahrendorf's trenchant and important 1979 Jean Monnet lecture.
'. . . given the technical structure of Community policies, and the mixture of institutional inertia and vested interests which upholds it, it is virtually impossible to see how Britain's understandable demands can be met. There are in fact only two ways of achieving the objective. One would be to increase the Community Budget by a considerable amount, such as 50 per cent, and thus make possible policies from which Britain would benefit more than others. This will not happen; indeed Britain itself will argue against any expansion of Community expenditure. The other is to slaughter the sacred cow and take at least some of the automaticity out of either the income or the expenditure side of agricultural trade and production'.

The Public Expenditure White Paper, 1980-81

The Government's long-term plans were disclosed in the Public Expenditure White Paper published with the Budget proposals on March 26, 1980. If nothing else, the 1980 Budget represented a milestone in British public finance; for the first time, expenditure and taxation proposals were published jointly, and for the first time monetary targets were set for several years ahead. Total government expenditure at constant prices (and the number of civil servants) rose during the first year of the Conservative Government, in spite of the 'cuts' – from £69.6bn to £69.9bn. However, a fall to £69.5bn is planned for 1980-81, followed by significant reductions thereafter, to 67.1bn in 1983-84.

Expenditure on all forms of regional and general industrial support also rose in 1979-80, but is planned to return to the 1978-9 figure in 1980-81 and thereafter to fall very sharply indeed, from just over £1bn in 1979-80 to just over half that figure in 1983-84. Expenditure on employment and training will fall in 1981-82 and thereafter, but scientific and technological assistance will rise. The longer-term plans therefore imply a reduction in the level of the industrial subsidies which expanded under the Labour Government, as well as a continuation of the fall in regional subsidies. However, these changes are due to take place in the period 1981 to 1983, which in politics is a long time ahead.

Table XVIII
GOVERNMENT EXPENDITURE
£ million at 1979 survey prices

	1978-79	1979-80	1980-81	1981-82	1982-83	1983-84
Regional and general industrial support	967	1,008	967	720	570	550
(of which regional develoment grants)	(404)	(304)	(337)			
Scientific and technological assistance	254	282	306	310	290	300
Employment and training	1,070	1,121	1,123	1,000	1,000	870
TOTAL Government Expenditure	69,611	69,900	69,501		68,700	67,100

Source: Public Expenditure White Paper, 1980-81.

Two recent developments would seem to illustrate the general issues discussed in the essay.

(1) The rise in unemployment to over 2 million has prompted calls for both a

Burmese solution' and a return to 'traditional' regional policy. (See the *Cambridge Economic Policy Review,* July 1980, and the *First Report on Welsh Affairs* of the House of Commons Select Committee on Welsh Affairs, Session 1979/1980.) Whether comprehensive import controls and 70 per cent tariffs would solve British problems cannot be discussed here; a good case can be made that they would not. Given for the time being, fairly high unemployment and low industrial profitability, neither 'traditional' regional policy, nor calls for workers to be more mobile, are likely to be very effective. Moreover, the issues which are giving rise to the greatest problems (e.g. the steel closures) affect *districts* rather than regions – Corby, Port Talbot, the Consett district – and not all of them are in Development Areas. For these *pointilliste* problems the kind of policy envisaged by the Government – action by the regional development agencies, re-training programmes, the encouragement of local entrepreneurship, the linking of Inmos's second £25 million to its setting up a factory on the other side of the Bristol Channel etc. – seems more appropriate than the kind of policy called for by Cambridge economists or Welsh MPs. The demand by the Welsh MPs that South Wales should not bear too much of the brunt of the BSC closures is perfectly reasonable regional lobbying – in which some hyperbole is taken for granted. (And one possible strategy, the closure of *both* the two main steelworks of South Wales, would have very serious consequences). But the Welsh MPs – and especially the Labour MPs among them – might well reflect that the present decision-making process is the consequence of steel production being controlled by a single centralised organisation. Under a more competitive system, the Welsh plants might well have fared better.

(2) The Local Government Planning and Land Bill represents an important change in the position of local government – probably the most important *constitutional* change which will be effected by the present Government. It has long been clear that the present rate support grant is unsatisfactory. However, the present Bill, which according to schedule will be an Act in the Autumn, has some of the characteristics familiar to students of legislation by Post-War Labour Governments, e.g. on the taxation of land values. Legislation on complex and far-reaching issues has been hurriedly drafted and insufficiently considered in detail, with its defects becoming apparent to civil servants, and possibly Ministers, only when the Government's prestige is committed to the Bill's passage. These failings arise from the unparalleled speed of the British law-making process, together with the 'mandate' doctrine. The drafting of the financial arrangements in the current Bill appears to have been dominated by the Government's desire to control what it saw as excessive spending by some local authorities, rather to the exclusion of longer term constitutional considerations. The present rate support system will be replaced by a new

'block grant', and the central government will, for the first time, have the power to limit local rate poundages. Few independent experts believe that the proposed system possesses the advantages claimed for it (see Tyrell Burgess and Tony Travers, *Ten Billion Pounds* Grant McIntyre, 1980), and there is no question that the power of Whitehall over local authorities will be further increased. Conservative, as well as Labour, local authorities opposed the Bill, but their objections had no effect. Great Britain, with no regional tier, and local authorities predominantly financed through Whitehall, now has the most centralised governmental system in Western Europe, and seems to have acquired it in a fit of absent-mindedness.

Notes

1. *The Economy of Cities*, 1970, p.89.

2. e.g. G. Cameron and L. Wingo, *Cities, Regions and Public Policy* (1973).

3. *Economic Policy Review*, Department of Applied Economics, Cambridge. March, 1978, p.7 ff.

4. Gunner Myrdal, *Economic Theory and Underdeveloped Regions*, 1957.

5. *Inner Area Studies. Summaries of consultants' final reports.* Dept. of the Environment, HMSO 1977. See the discussion below.

6. An exposition of neo-Marxist thought on regional policy – by 'an economist who has been influential in formulating British Government policies' – is *Capital versus the Regions* by Stuart Holland, 1976.

7. See Samuel Brittan, *Second Thoughts on Full Employment*, Centre for Policy Studies, 1974.

8. 'Evaluating the effects of British Regional Economic Policy' *Economic Journal*, March 1973.

9. Harvey Armstrong and Jim Taylor, *Regional Economic Policy and its Analysis*, Philip Allan, 1978.

10. The latest guide to the multifarious subsidies available in the Special Development Areas, Development Areas, and Intermediate Areas refers to them as 'the areas of high labour supply': *Incentives for Industry in the Areas for Expansion*, Department of Industry, 1978, p.5.

11. This problem is also raised in wider issues of economic policy. The economists who attribute the decline in British regional differences to "regional policy", on the basis of temporal coincidence, often defend the policies that have been pursued since 1973 – price control, incomes policy, industrial subsidy – on the grounds that a mere reliance on fiscal and monetary policy would lead to higher unemployment. But Britain has since 1973 experienced *higher* unemployment than OECD countries which have relied on fiscal and monetary policy. This temporal coincidence is again not proof of a causal relationship, but one ought not to cite coincidence as proof of a causal relationship only when it suits one's argument. As David Hume pointed out two hundred years ago – causal relationships can be, provisionally, established only by postulating a casual (i.e. micro-economic and macro-economic) data. Many sophisticated University economists appear to have lost sight of this fundamental scientific principle.

12. P.M. Townroe *Industrial Location Decisions*, Occasional Paper 15. Centre for Urban and Regional Studies, University of Birmingham, 1971.

13. P. Gripaios, 'The closure of firms in the inner city: the south-east London case 1970-75. *Regional Studies*, Vol.11 No.1, 1977.

14. N. Mobbs, *The inner city – a location for industry?* Slough Estates Ltd., 1977.

15. R.D. Dennis 'The decline of manufacturing employment in Greater London, 1966-74. *Urban Studies*, Vol.15, 1978, p.63.

16. The argument was based on the results of a survey which seemed to show that many firms were basing investment decisions on estimated returns *before* tax allowances. This was interpreted as a failure to understand the principles of elementary profit-and-loss accounting. Is it not conceivable, however, that – in an age of inflation and erratic government policy – it was a rational procedure?

17. P.M. Townroe *Industrial Location Decisions* op.cit., p.83.

18. O.E.C.D. studies of the real return on capital indicate that, whereas in most countries there has been a slight downward trend since 1960, at around 12%, the figure for the UK fell from an unusually low 5 per cent to an unprecedented low of 2 per cent in 1975. (*Towards Full Employment and Price Stability*, 1977, p.305). Bank of England calculations give higher recent figures, with a recovery from 3.5 per cent in 1975 to 4 per cent in 1977, but the same general movements (*Quarterly Bulletin*, Dec. 1978). A different indicator is gross profits as a percentage of national income: the British figure, 5.2 per cent, was the lowest among industrial countries in 1978 (*United Kingdom – O.E.C.D. Survey*, March 1979).

19. *Regional Policy for Ever?* IEA Readings II, Institute of Economic Affairs, London 1973.

20. *Work for Wales*, Bow Group Pamphlet, 1959.

21. 'What is the answer?' No one gathered around her bed spoke. 'In that case, what is the question?'.

22. The direct contribution by the IEA (or its Editor) was confined to the title, some signed footnotes, and an admirable use of the red pencil on verbiage. The author of a detailed study of EEC policy misinterpreted the authorship and purpose of the booklet and, I suspect, the implication of the title, when he wrote: 'The IEA in London levelled some telling blows against the Community's regional policy in general but even the IEA viewed the chances of defeating the proposals as so minimal that it entitled its interesting and provocative volume '*Regional Policy for Ever?*' (Ross B. Talbot, 'The European Community's Regional Fund'. Progress in Planning, Vol.8, 113, p.263.

23. Stanley Katz. *The Birmingham Post*, 31st May, 1973.

24. Quoted in N. Lichfield. *Economics of Planned Development* (1955) p.366.

25. 'Regional planning in Britain', by Maurice Wright and Stephen Young in *Planning, Politics and Public Policy* by Jack Hayward and Michael Watson (eds.) C.U.P. 1975.

26. G. Hallett, *Urban Land Economics*, MacMillan 1979, Chap. 11.

27. G. Manners, 'Reinterpreting the regional problem'. *Three Banks Review*, September, 1976.

28. M. Chisholm, 'Regional Policies in an era of slow population growth and higher unemployment' *Regional Studies* 10, 1976. M. Chisholm and J. Oeppen. *The Changing Pattern of Employment, Regional Specialisation and Industrial Localisation in Britain*, Croom Helm 1973.

29. *Inner Area Studies: Summaries of consultants' final reports*, Department of the Environment, 1977. HMSO £1.50 p.3.

30. For a detailed examination see Max Wilkinson, *Lessons from Europe*. A Comparison of British and West European Schooling, Centre for Policy Studies, 1977.

31. See the article by Professor James M. Buchanan in *The Economics of Politics* IEA Readings 18, Institute of Economic Affairs, London, 1978. Many proponents of the 'public choice' school suggest that politicians are *purely* self-seeking, which seems to me to be a little *too* Machiavellian. The 'public choice' school is a salutary corrective to the Benthamite-Fabian school, which overlooks the possibility of administrative and political imperfections and has dominated British post-war policy, but it also needs to be taken with a pinch of salt. I discuss these questions in *Urban Land Economics*, Macmillan, 1979, p.31 ff.

32. See *Gilding the Ghetto* and *Profits versus Houses*, the Community Development Project, published by the Home Office, London.

33. I examine Professor Harvey's views more fully in Chapter 7 of *Urban Land Economics: Principles and Policy*, Macmillan, 1979.

34. N.J. Fores, 'No More General Theories?' *Economic Journal*, March 1969.

35. A. Lindbeck. *The Political Economy of the New Left*. 1971, p.39.

36. Probably still the best examination of the role and limitations of economic planning – the conclusions of which have been ignored in subsequent planning ventures – is a report for the Fabian Society (W.A. Lewis, *Principles of Economic Planning*, Allen & Unwin, 1949).

37. This point emerges from the chapters by the more historically-minded contributors – especially Professor Vaizey and David Law – in a symposium on Irish economic problems (*Economic Sovereignty and Regional Policy*). John Vaizey (ed.), MacMillan and Gill, Dublin, (1975).

38. *Capitalism, Socialism and Democracy*, 1940. p.81 ff.

39. Reprinted in *Capitalism and the Permissive Society*, Macmillan, 1973, p.249.

40. Under the 'universal banking system, which played such an important role in German industrialisation and in the post-1945 recovery of the Federal Republic, the banks have representatives on the boards of companies to which they lend money. The banks closely monitor firms' financial performance and usually insist on corrective action when it is needed. When firms get into real difficulties, the banks take a long view. British commercial banks, by contrast, have on several occasions taken no action as firms have got into difficulties, but have then bankrupted them by calling in overdrafts. The Fairey Group, now earning large profits for the NEB, two years after bankruptcy, is a case in point. Even those who reject Labour Party proposals for nationalising the banks can feel that there is scope for an improvement in their relations with industry, and some kind of public or semi-public 'presence' in the financial sector.

41. The issues are, however, related. The form of nationalisation traditionally favoured by the Labour Party – the control of a whole industry by a single monolithic organisation – is peculiarly well adapted to the exercise of political intervention. In other European countries, public ownership tends to take different forms – such as a nationalised firm in competition with private firms (the steel industry) or a shareholding by central or regional government (Volkswagen). Cooperatives and other non-profit enterprises are also far more important. In Great Britain, the idea of industrial cooperatives has recently been harmed by the nature of its sponsors and by large subsidies for badly managed enterprises. The situation is very different in, for example, West Germany. The largest construction firm (*Neue Heimat*) is owned by the trade union federation, and non-profit enterprises of all types are successful and – as both supporters and opponents agree – essential elements in the 'socially responsible market economy'.

42. For an excellent account of Italian economic problems see Giselle Podbielski, *Italy*, Oxford University Press, 1974.

43. 'The End of Laissez-faire' in *Essays in Persuasion*. Macmillan for the Royal Economic Society, 1972, p.290.

44. Colin Clark, "Industrial Location and Economic Potential'. Lloyds Bank Review. October, 1966.

45. *Regional Policy for Ever?* p.87.

46. I have examined the curious history of British land taxation in Pt. III of *Housing and Land Policies in West Germany and Britain* (Macmillan, 1977).

47. *Housing and Land Policies in West Germany and Britain*, pp 73-75, 83-88.

48. *Parliamentary Debates (Commons) 1973-4*, 4 April Col.1441.

49. G.N. Mobbs. *The Inner City – A Location for Industry?* – Slough Estates Ltd., 1977.

50. 'British Government and Politics'. Lecture at the London School of Economics, 10 May, 1979.

51. *Development Planning* p.67. But there is no need to throw the baby out with the bath water. Economic development remains a reasonable goal for the 'Third World', and the older insights have been incorporated into some of the latest books on the subject. e.g. Michael P. Todaro, *Economic Development in the Third World*, New York, 1977.

52. J. Salt, 'The impact of the Ford and Vauxhall plants on the unemployment situation of Merseyside, 1962-1965'. *Tijdschrift voor Economische en Sociale Geografie* 58, p.255-64.

53. As Professor West points out (*Regional Policy for Ever?* op.cit., p.110).

54. For a political scientist's astonished survey of welfare economics and cost-benefit analysis, see Peter Self, *Econocrats and the Policy Process*, Macmillan, 1975.

55. *The Theory of Economic Growth*, p.408.

56. Supplement 8/73. *Bulletin of the European Committees.*

57. Ross B. Talbot. *The European Community's Regional Fund*, Progress in Planning, Vol.8, Part 3. Pergamon Press, 1977).

58. The Thomson Report stated that the average income of the richest regions was about five times that the poorest, and that this ratio had remained unaltered since the formation of the Community. The McDougal Report gives a figure of four times for 1970. But international income comparisons (e.g. Paris with Calabria) are well-known to be problematical, and to overstate real differences.

59. This use of the term 'sub-region' probably implies an American scale, on which the whole of Great Britain would be considered a 'region'. It is not the sense in which the term is used by British writers.

60. G. Hallett 'Regional Policies in the European Economic Community' in *Regional Policy for Ever?* 1973, p.59.

61. *Report of the Study Group on the Role of Public Finance in European Integration*, 1977. (Chairman, Sir Robert McDougal).

62. The income differences between states, with Alaska having the highest average income, illustrates the textbook point about the difficulty of using international income differences as an indicator of living standards in real terms. Presumably, some of the higher income in Alaska goes in coping with the relatively high costs of living there.

3. Some figures from a Commission working document were leaked. The Budget Commissioner then released official figures, which were withdrawn the next day because some agricultural items had been added instead of subtracted! The figures given were said to be 'definitive'.

4. In the Spring of 1979, the European Parliament sought to raise farm prices by more than the amount proposed by the Commission. However, the drafters of the resolution were confused by the intricacies of the Common Agricultural Policy and referred to the wrong unit of account. In consequence, the resolution, which was thought to call for a 3 per cent rise, actually called for a 17 per cent reduction. The new elected Parliament has taken a very different line from the old nominated Parliament, and sought to reduce agricultural support. This is an important change, which increases the political forces in favour of a more rational agricultural policy.

5. A periodical in which James Madison and others examine the principles on which the U.S. Constitution should be based. Very little of the mass of literature on the EEC is of comparable calibre. The current rather disillusioned state of the Community is perhaps an appropriate time to go back to first principles and ask 'What functions of government are necessary at all? What can be left at the local level, what must be conducted at the regional, the national, the Community or a wider level?

6. For a general discussion of the methodology of economics, which points in a similar direction, see T.W. Hutchinson, *On Revolutions and Progress in Economic Knowledge*, CUP, 1978.

7. One of the best textbooks, free from any of the criticisms levelled above at British regional economics, is *An Introduction to Regional Economics*, by E.M. Hoover, New York, 1971.

8. R.T. Ely and G.S. Wehrwein, *Land Economics*, Wisconsin University Press, 1940.

9. The term 'traditional' is used to indicate the policy adopted in the 1950s and 1960s. It does not mean that this policy derives from a long tradition of economic thought.

70. W. Bahr and P. Friedrich (eds.), *Competition among Small Regions*. Nomos Verlag, Baden-Baden, 1978.

71. I am indebted in this section to a lecture by Dr Hans-Jürgen Ewers, Deputy Director, International Institute of Management.

72. Graham Bannock, *The Smaller Business in Britain and Germany*, Wilton House for the Anglo-German Foundation, London, 1976.

73. David L. Birch. *The Job Generation Process*, MIT Program on Neighbourhood and Regional Change, Cambridge, Mass. 1979.
There has been some questioning whether these findings, or the author's conclusions, apply to the UK. It would certainly be unwise to swing from a rather uncritical belief in bigness to an equally uncritical belief in smallness. The most important lesson of this and similar studies is rather the high level of growth and death of jobs, and the need for conditions in which the growth of jobs can flourish.

74. See R.L.G. McKie, *Planning from the Bottom Up*, Queens University, Belfast. New Lecture Series 107, 1977.

75. This section draws on the ideas of Professor C. Freeman, of the Science Policy Research Unit, University of Sussex.

76. For an excellent discussion of the subject see *Devolution* by Vernon Bogdanor, Oxford University Press, 1979.

77. Lord Kilbrandon (Chairman), *Royal Commission on the Constitution* 1969-73. Memorandum of Dissent by Professor Peacock and Lord Crowther-Hunt.

78. *Devolution: The English Dimension. A Consultative Document.* HMSO, 1976.

79. *Report of the Committee of Enquiry on Local Government Finance.* Cmnd 6453.

80. Lord Hailsham. *Dilemma of Democracy: Diagnosis and Prescription*, 1977.

(I) e.g. in the latest symposium, *Regional Policy: Past Experience and New Directions*, ed. Duncan MacLennan and John D. Parr, Martin Robertson, 1979.

(II) See Graham Hallett, *Housing and Land Policy in West Germany and Britain*, Macmillan, Pt.3. 1977, pt.3.

(III)But for an alternative view see 'NEB: A Case for Euthanasia', M. Grylls and J. Redwood, CPS, 1980.